CONTENTS

FREAKY PEAKS

INTRODUCTION

Like everything else in life, geography has its ups and downs. Take lessons about monstrous mountains, for instance. One minute you're sitting at your desk, your head in the clouds, daydreaming about being famous, while your geography teacher drones on and on...

Next thing you know, your dreams are shattered. Your teacher's voice brings you down to Earth with a bang. Yep, it's all downhill from now on.

NEXT WEEK'S LESSON IS ABOUT OROGENY.* FOR THE FIELD TRIP ON THURSDAY, YOU'LL NEED A ROPE, A CRASH HELMET, WARM CLOTHES, THICK SOCKS, STURDY BOOTS, A TENT, A PACKED LUNCH, SOME GOGGLES, SOME GLOVES, BLAH, BLAH, BLAH...

WAAAAAAAH!

Where on Earth are you going?

* Oro–jen–ee is the technical term for the way freaky peaks are formed. It comes from two old Greek words for "mountain" and "born". In other words, your teacher's telling you you've got a mountain to climb. Don't freak out. If even climbing out of bed in the morning makes you go wobbly and weak at the knees, why not try this impressive-sounding excuse. Put up your hand, look peaky, and say:

** Being acrophobic (ak–row–foe–bick) means being scared of heights. It comes from another old Greek word for "peaky" or "high up". And the freaky Greeks knew all about peaks. After all, they lived in one of the hilliest places on Earth.

If, on the other hand, you're the sort of person who thinks climbing mountains sounds dead exciting but you can't be bothered to go outside, try this simple indoor experiment. Walk up and down stairs ten times on the trot. Go on, you can do it. If your grown-ups complain you'll wear out the carpet, smile sweetly and explain – you're climbing the stairs because they are there. You're in good company. That's why one famous climber said he climbed Mount Everest – because it was there! Your grown-ups will be much too mystified to moan.

And that's what this book is all about. Higher than the world's tallest skyscraper, as old as the hills and as icy as the poles, *Freaky Peaks* will have you clinging on for dear life. You can...

• scale the dizzy heights of the world's top peaks with Cliff, your trusty mountain guide.

• join the hunt for the hard-to-get yeti (if it exists).

- search for fossil seashells on top of the world (it's true).

- learn how to live through an avalanche (against the odds).

This is geography like never before. And it's horribly gripping. But be warned – don't read this book on your freaky field trip halfway up a mountain. Otherwise, as you're turning the page, you might just fall off the edge…

ON TOP OF THE WORLD

29 May 1953, Mount Everest, Nepal

4 a.m. Dawn was breaking over Mount Everest, the highest place on Earth, bathing the peaks for miles around in a rosy glow. In a tiny, wind-battered tent, precariously perched on a rocky ledge, two men were in the middle of the biggest adventure of their lives.

They were attempting to reach the top of the world, and earn a place in history. Both of them knew they might die trying. No human being had climbed so high before. No one knew if you even could. But it was a risk they were willing to take.

The two men in question were Edmund Hillary and Tenzing Norgay. Back home in New Zealand, Hillary worked in the family bee-keeping business. He'd only been climbing for six short years, though he'd already been to Mount Everest. Norgay was a very experienced Sherpa climber from Nepal, born and raised in the mountains. The year before, he'd climbed to a staggering 8,595 metres up the mountain before fierce winds and freezing cold weather had forced him back. It had been a superhuman effort. But now he was back on Everest, determined to go one better. The two men made a formidable team. Both were tough, brave

11

and fighting fit. Given what lay in store for them, they'd need all these gritty qualities.

They were now in their ninth and final camp, some 8,370 metres up the mountain, having left Camp 8 the day before. Poking their heads anxiously out of the tent door, the men saw that the weather looked fine and settled. For now, at least. The howling wind which had kept them awake most of the night was mercifully still. Even so, the temperature inside their tent had plummeted to an icy –27°C, so bitterly cold that their leather boots had frozen solid. While they had breakfast (tea, lemon juice, biscuits and sardines), Hillary heated the boots slowly over the portable stove to thaw them out.

An hour or so later, after a last, quick check of their oxygen tanks, ropes and ice axes – three crucial pieces of their equipment – they were finally ready to go. At 6.30 a.m., Tenzing and Hillary crawled out of the little tent and set off for their final assault on the summit.

Taking turns to lead, the plucky pair began their long, slow climb towards the South Summit (a peak before the main summit). The first obstacle facing them was a narrow, rocky ridge with sheer drops on either side. Crossing it took great strength and courage. But somehow they made it. No sooner were they safely across than a new hazard loomed. To reach the South Summit, they needed to climb a steep slope of snow. Normally, it was straightforward to cut steps in snow using an ice axe. But here the snow was fine and powdery and covered by an icy crust. It felt like walking on broken eggshells. For every five steps the men climbed, they slid back three as the fragile surface crumbled beneath their feet. Climbing the slippery slope was going to be horribly risky but they knew they could not give up now. They'd come too far for that. Hearts pounding, the two men pressed on and at 9 a.m. they finally reached the South Summit.

Even now, there was no time to relax. Another ridge, sharp as a knife, loomed ahead of them. On one side hung billowing sheets of snow, like massive, icy curtains. Below them lay a sheer drop. On the other side was a huge bank of snow sloping steeply down to a wall of bare, grey rock. It was vital to concentrate now. One false step and they'd surely plummet to their deaths. Roped together for safety, they picked their way gingerly across the snow.

This time, luckily, it was hard and firm and they were able to keep their footing. Step after agonizing step they climbed on, their bodies straining with the effort. A niggling worry lodged in their minds. They had enough oxygen left in their tanks for another four and a half hours. Would that be enough to reach the summit and get back down again? Only time would tell. But without oxygen, they would never make it.

The summit of Everest now looked tantalizingly close. But in the mountains, distances can be deceptive. There were still several hours of hard climbing to go. And now a truly awesome obstacle blocked their path – a vast, vertical step of rock, rising more than 12 metres high, right across the ridge.

Their hearts sank. The rock face was so steep and sheer there was simply no way of climbing it. Was this the end? Surely, they'd have to turn back now? Then, to the right of the step, they spotted a narrow crack snaking between the rock and a huge icy overhang (technically called a cornice). This was their only chance. Clinging on for dear life, Hillary wedged himself into the crack and hauled himself up, inch by painstaking inch, using his knees, elbows, shoulders and ice axe. If the ice gave way, as it could anytime, he would plunge to his death on the glacier below.

They were nail-biting minutes. Finally, to Tenzing's great relief, Hillary appeared on a wide ledge at the top of the crack. Now it was Tenzing's turn to follow. So far, so good. But the effort of this nerve-jangling climb had cost the two men dear. For now, they collapsed in exhaustion on the ledge, glad to still be alive. But their minds were made up. They were more determined now than ever before. Whatever else the mountain threw at them, nothing could stop them now.

For two more hours, the men hacked their way upwards, each step a superhuman effort. In the thin mountain air, each breath became harder and harder. It seemed like an endless task. Slowly but surely, their new-found determination began to drain away. Would they ever reach the summit? Then, just above them, they saw a small, snow-covered hump about the size of a haystack. It could have been an icy rock anywhere in the world. Except for one thing – this one was 8,848 metres high. At long, long last, this was the summit of Mount Everest and their journey's end. At 11.30 a.m., on 29 May 1953, five long hours after leaving Camp 9, Edmund Hillary and Tenzing Norgay found themselves standing on top of the world.

Delightedly, the two men shook hands and hugged each other with joy. After all the years of planning and all the failed expeditions, they'd finally made it to the top. There was no need to say anything. Words simply could not express how they both felt. Hillary pulled out his camera and snapped Tenzing waving the flags of Britain, Nepal, India and the United Nations.

Then Tenzing dug a small hole in the snow and buried a pencil, a black cloth cat and some sweets and biscuits, offerings to the mountain gods for guiding them to safety. Alongside them, Hillary buried a crucifix. Then it was time to admire the view. A view no human being had ever seen before – a breathtaking scene of scudding clouds, snow-capped peaks, snaking valleys and glistening glaciers. But their time on the summit could only be short. To save enough oxygen for the descent, they could only stay for 15 minutes. Then it was time for them to go back down to the rest of the expedition, anxiously waiting at the lower camps. Time to come back down to Earth.

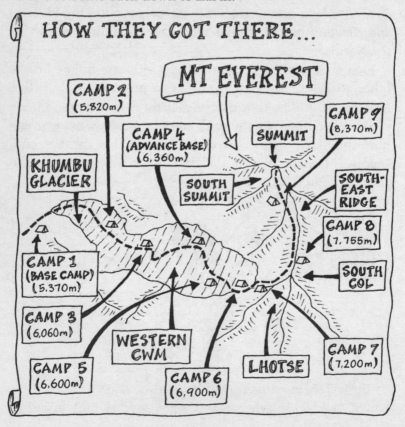

Freaky peak fact file

NAME: Mount Everest

LOCATION: Tibet/Nepal

HEIGHT: 8,848 m

AGE: about 40 million years old

PEAK TYPE: Fold (see page 24)

PEAKY POINTS:

- The highest mountain on Earth.
- It's part of the Himalayas, the highest mountain range.
- It was named after Sir George "Never-rest" Everest (1790–1866), the first person to measure the mountain. He got his nickname for being such a slave-driver. Before this, Mount Everest was boringly called Peak XV.
- It's also called Chomolungma (Mother Goddess of the World) and Sagarmatha (Goddess of the Sky).

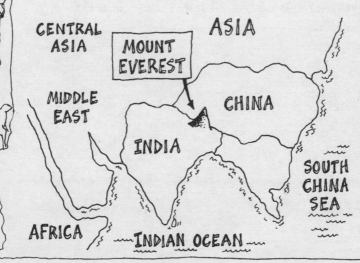

CENTRAL ASIA

ASIA

MOUNT EVEREST

MIDDLE EAST

CHINA

INDIA

SOUTH CHINA SEA

AFRICA

INDIAN OCEAN

So horrible humans had finally gone completely over the top. And Tenzing and Hillary became superstars. They were showered with prizes and top honours (Hillary was made a knight and Tenzing was given the George Medal). Since their record-breaking climb, hundreds of brave (or barmy?) climbers have followed in their footsteps. So if you've got a good head for heights and fancy the adventure of a lifetime, why not face up to a freaky peak of your own? If Everest looks a wee bit scary for starters, don't worry. There are plenty more mountains to climb.

HORRIBLE HEALTH WARNING

Climbing mountains can be horribly dangerous, as you've already seen. So don't go trying it on your own – take a qualified mountaineer with you. Always check the weather before you set out – mountain weather can quickly turn nasty. And always let someone know where you're going and how long you think you're going to be so they can send for help.

MOVING MOUNTAINS

Ask someone to think of a mountain, and they'll most likely describe a boring block of rotten rock, shaped a bit like a pyramid. But there's much more to freaky peaks than that. Honestly! Ask any horrible geographer. (Be warned – geographers love the sound of their own voices. You might be in for a horribly long-winded answer.) They'll tell you freaky peaks cover a fifth of the Earth's surface. That's an awful lot of mountain! But what are freaky peaks and how on Earth did they get there? And why on Earth are they so horribly high? Here's a handy map of some of the highest...

What on Earth are freaky peaks?

Strictly speaking, a mountain's a steep-sided rock that rises above the Earth's surface. (Oh, you knew that already?) You measure a mountain by its height above sea level. Even if it's nowhere near the sea. Confusing, eh? Some geographers think proper peaks must be at least 1,000 metres high (that's like three Eiffel Towers plonked on top of each other) if you're going to call them mountains. Others say any old (large-ish) hill or hump will do.

For hundreds of years, mountains had geographers mystified. They knew freaky peaks existed (OK, so you don't have to be a brain surgeon to work that out) but they couldn't agree how they'd got there. Here are some of their over-the-top theories…

According to English vicar Thomas Burnet (1635–1715) the Earth's surface was once as smooth as an eggshell. But God wanted to punish people for their sins. So he cracked the shell open and water poured out. (Remember Noah and the Ark? This is the flood that made them famous.) The slivers of smashed-up shell became mountains. It might sound weird to us now. But astonishingly, a hundred years later, Thomas's eggy theory was still going strong.

Meanwhile, top Scottish geographer James Hutton (1726–1797) had other ground-breaking ideas. He reckoned (rightly) that peaks were pushed up over millions of years by natural forces which twisted and bent the rocks. But he couldn't say what these freaky forces were. James wrote his ideas down in a long, boring book called *Theory of the Earth*. Unfortunately, very few people bothered to read it because his writing was so hard to understand. Besides, they liked the flood story better.

And it didn't stop there. American geologist James Dwight Dana (1813–1895) claimed the Earth was once a red-hot ball of soft, squishy rock. As it cooled, it shrank, and its surface went all dry and wrinkly (like skin on cold school custard. Yuk. Or your fingers in the bath.). The wrinkly bits were freaky peaks. Simple as that.

It seemed that every geographer worth his or her salt had something to say. But, guess what? They still couldn't say exactly how mountains were made. Freaky peaks had them well and truly stumped.

Teacher teaser
Forgotten to do your geography homework? Why not sidetrack your teacher with this painful question:

What on Earth are you talking about?

Answer: No, mountains don't go to the dentist. Lucky things. But your question's not as silly as it seems. You see, British geographer Sir George Airy (1801–1892) reckoned mountains were a bit like teeth. Freaky peaks were the bits you see (like your gleaming, pearly-white gnashers giving a cheesy grin). But underneath they'd got huge, long, rocky roots reaching down into the ground (just like the roots that hold your teeth in your jaw and stop them falling out). Had brilliant but barmy Sir George bitten off more than he could chew? No, he was right.

Earth-moving ideas
But it wasn't until 1910 that geographers finally got to the root of the peaky problem. Then brilliant German geographer Alfred Wegener (1880–1930) had a brainwave. He worked out that the Earth's rocky surface (called the crust – that's the bit of the Earth right beneath your feet) wasn't anything to do with eggshells or custard. Thank

goodness for that. Nope. Instead, the rock was cracked into lots of pieces, called plates, a bit like crazy paving (only on a seriously gigantic scale). There were seven huge chunks and lots of smaller ones. But get this: the plates didn't stay put in one place all the time. They were constantly on the move.

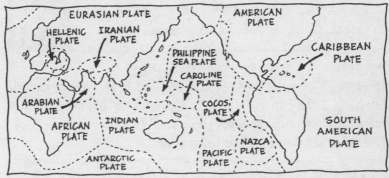

Brainy Alfred called his earth-shattering theory "continental drift". But he couldn't work out what made the plates move. Modern geographers now know the plates float on a layer of hot, gooey rock called magma. It's found underneath the crust (in a layer called the mantle). It's thick and sticky, a bit like treacle. Heat from deep inside the Earth churns up the magma and keeps the crusty plates on their toes.

Normally, the plates drift about without you even noticing. But sometimes, they get in each other's way. Some bash straight into each other. Others try to push and shove their way past. And guess what? Yep, this is how mighty mountains are made. The mystery was over.

Note: Sadly, nobody believed a word Alfred said. They dismissed his theory as claptrap. It was another 50 years before geographers finally proved, beyond any doubt, that the continents have drifted for millions of years and, what's more, they are still going. (Unfortunately, Alfred died before he could see his idea proved right.)

Spotter's guide to mountains

It's true, all freaky peaks are rocky and high but they're all horribly different. So if you're thinking of heading for the hills, why not sneak a quick peak in Cliff's useful guidebook. It'll fill you in on the four main types.

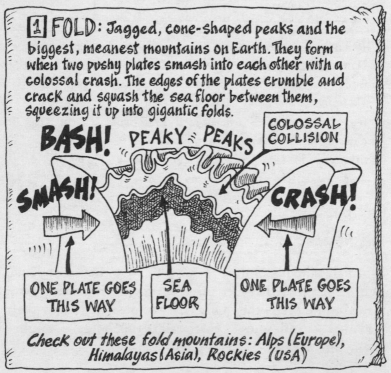

1 FOLD: Jagged, cone-shaped peaks and the biggest, meanest mountains on Earth. They form when two pushy plates smash into each other with a colossal crash. The edges of the plates crumble and crack and squash the sea floor between them, squeezing it up into gigantic folds.

BASH! PEAKY PEAKS
COLOSSAL COLLISION
SMASH!
CRASH!
ONE PLATE GOES THIS WAY
SEA FLOOR
ONE PLATE GOES THIS WAY

Check out these fold mountains: Alps (Europe), Himalayas (Asia), Rockies (USA)

Are you brave enough to make a freaky fold mountain?

Find out how fold mountains form with this simple but succulent experiment. Then you can eat it for lunch!

What you need:
- four slices of bread
- some marg or butter
- some hard cheese and peanut butter

What you do:

1 Make some nice, thick sandwiches (for the plates of the Earth's crust) with layers of butter, cheese and peanut butter (for the different layers of rocks).

2 Cut the sandwiches in half.

3 Take a sandwich in either hand and squidge them together. (Don't squidge too hard or you'll end up with a soggy mess.)

What happens?

a) your mum tells you off for making a mess

b) the dog steals your sandwiches

c) the sandwiches get squeezed upwards

Answer: c) Congratulations! You've made your own mountains. OK, so you'll need to use your imagination to get the idea. Lucky you didn't have to wait around for the real thing. They take millions and millions of years to form.

ER... I'M MAKING FREAKY PEAKS

YOU'RE THE ONE WHO'S FREAKY

2 BLOCK: Huge, wedge-shaped peaks which form at faults (they're giant cracks in the crust where two plates meet). As the drifting plates shift, they shove a great slab of rock up in between them. (Sometimes the slab sinks down instead and makes a vast, steep-sided valley.)

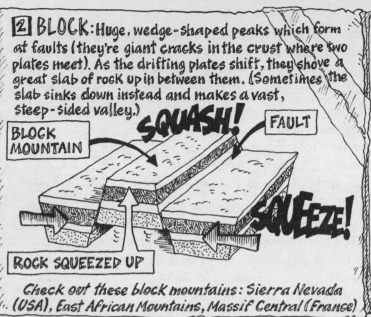

BLOCK MOUNTAIN

SQUASH!

FAULT

SQUEEZE!

ROCK SQUEEZED UP

Check out these block mountains: Sierra Nevada (USA), East African Mountains, Massif Central (France)

3 DOME: Round, hump-shaped hills. They're made by magma deep underground seeping to the surface. If the crust's too hard to crack, the magma shoves it into a dome-shaped bulge.
Dome mountains slope quite gently but can measure hundreds of kilometres around their base.

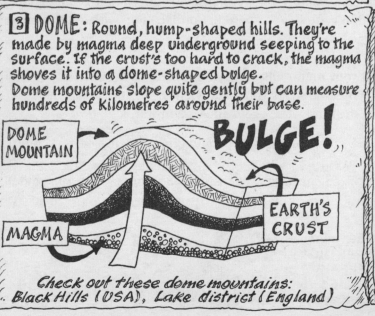

DOME MOUNTAIN

BULGE!

MAGMA

EARTH'S CRUST

Check out these dome mountains: Black Hills (USA), Lake district (England)

26

4 **VOLCANOES:** Steep, cone-shaped peaks. Volcanoes happen when red-hot magma spurts through a crack in the Earth's crust. It cools and hardens into rock which builds into a mountain. Some of the world's highest mountains are rumbling volcanoes. Don't panic, it's been a long time since these freaky peaks last blew their tops.

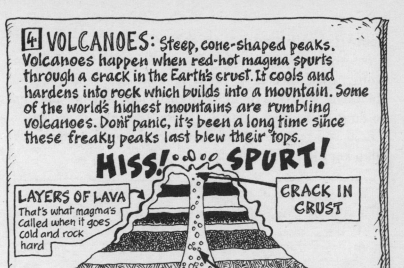

HISS! SPURT!

LAYERS OF LAVA
That's what magma's called when it goes cold and rock hard

CRACK IN CRUST

MAGMA RISING

Check out these volcanoes: Mount Kilimanjaro (Africa), Mount Elbruz (Russia)

Earth-shattering fact
Name three things you'd expect to find on top of a mountain. There's snow, of course. And lots of rock. There's even the odd jellyfish. That's right, jellyfish! You see, millions of years ago freaky fold mountains were part of the ancient sea floor. So you often find fossils of seashells, jellyfish and other sea animals wedged in the rocks. For years, people thought they'd been stuck there deliberately as a peaky practical joke!

Could you be a geologist?

Ever wondered what on Earth mountains are made from? Rotten rock, of course. Some horrible geographers spend their lives studying rocks. (It's a hard job but someone's got to do it.) The posh name for these rock docs is geologists. Could you be a stony-faced geologist? You'll need a rock-solid knowledge of rocks first.

Getting to know your rock isn't as hard as it sounds. Just remember, all the rocks on Earth belong to one of these three groups. . .

A: SEDIMENTARY ROCKS

HOW FORMED: from tiny fragments of rock, sand or the skeletons of tiny sea creatures, squashed and squeezed into solid layers of rock. Over millions of years, the sea creatures turn into fossils.

ROCKY TYPES: limestone, sandstone, dolomite.

PEAKY SITES: Alps, Himalayas, Jura (Europe)

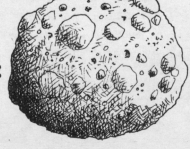

B: *IGNEOUS ROCKS*

HOW FORMED: from red-hot rocks chucked out of violent volcanoes (that's why they're also called fire rocks), which cool and harden in the air.

ROCKY TYPES:
basalt, andesite, granite.

PEAKY SITES:
Andes, Rockies, Sierra Nevada (USA)

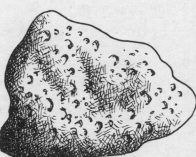

C: *METAMORPHIC ROCKS*

HOW FORMED: from sedimentary or igneous rocks cooked by heat from volcanoes or crushed by the forces that build freaky peaks so they change into different rocks altogether.

ROCKY TYPES:
marble, schist, gneiss.

PEAKY SITES:
Alps, Appennines (Italy) Appalachians (USA)

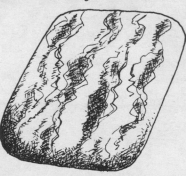

1. BASALT
A SMOOTH, DARK ROCK STUDDED WITH GREEN CRYSTALS. AND THE COMMONEST ROCK ON EARTH.

2. GRANITE
A POLISHED BLEND OF PINKY GREY ROCK AND QUARTZ CRYSTALS. TOUGH BUT TASTY.

3. ANDESITE
SPRINKLED WITH SPECKLES OF BROWN AND GREY, A REAL TASTE OF THE ANDES. (THAT'S HOW IT GETS ITS NAME).

4. LIMESTONE
LAYERS OF LIGHT BROWN AND GREY ROCK, FILLED WITH YUMMY FOSSIL SEA CREATURES.

5. DOLOMITE
GREY AND CRUNCHY WITH A CRYSTAL CENTRE. YOU'LL WANT A WHOLE MOUNTAIN NEXT. (HEAD FOR THE DOLOMITES IN EUROPE IF YOU DO).

6. SANDSTONE
A GRITTY MIXTURE OF SUMPTUOUS SAND GRAINS. MIND IT DOESN'T STICK IN YOUR TEETH.

7. GNEISS (NICE)
TASTY LAYERS OF LIGHT AND DARK ROCK, WITH A CRUNCHY TWIST. GNEISS BY NAME AND NICE BY NATURE.

8. SCHIST
A FLAKY FEAST, THE LITTLE RED BITS ARE GORGEOUS GARNETS (YOU CAN USE THEM TO MAKE GEOLOGICAL JEWELLERY).

9. MARBLE
PURE WHITE AND CRUMBLY, WITH A TEXTURE LIKE SUGAR, OR HARD AND STREAKED WITH GREY, PINK OR GREEN. A REALLY CLASSY ROCK CHOC.

10. SLATE
GREY AND MADE FROM THE FINEST MUDSTONE. EASY TO CUT INTO SLICES.

LOOKING FOR THAT EXTRA-SPECIAL PRESENT?

FED UP WITH FLOWERS AND SMELLY SOAP?

Look no further...

FOR THE PERFECT GIFT TO WOW YOUR TEACHER AND IMPRESS YOUR FRIENDS, CHECK OUT A BOX OF OUR NEW, IMPROVED*...

Rotten Rock Chocs

The sweet that'll set your teeth on edge!

GO ON, DIG IN...

*Now with even greater crunchiness!

WARNING! MIND YOUR TEETH WHEN YOU'RE MUNCHING THESE CHOCCIES. THEY'VE GOT HORRIBLY HARD CENTRES.

31

Freaky peak facts

Is your geography teacher at the peak of her powers? Find out with this freaky True/False quiz.

1 Mount Everest is the highest mountain on Earth. TRUE/FALSE?

2 Mount Everest is the tallest mountain on Earth. TRUE/FALSE?

3 The Himalayas are the longest mountain range. TRUE/FALSE?

4 Mountains grow under the sea. TRUE/FALSE?

5 Most mountains are less than 1,000 years old. TRUE/FALSE?

6 There aren't any mountains in Britain. TRUE/FALSE?

Answers:

1 TRUE. At a staggering 8,848 metres high, Everest's officially the highest peak on the planet. It's almost 20 times higher than the world's highest skyscraper. Or as high as your house ... with another 599 houses on top.

What's more, Everest's still growing. It's true. That's because the two crusty plates that pushed up the Himalayas are still smashing away. Experts reckon Everest's getting about 13 millimetres higher every year. Doesn't sound much, but that makes it more than 50 centimetres higher than it was in Tenzing and Hillary's day.

2 FALSE. Everest may be the world's highest peak if you measure it from sea level. But it certainly isn't the tallest. The world-record holder's Mauna Kea in Hawaii. Measured from its bottom, deep under the sea, this vast volcano's an awesome 10,203 metres tall, beating Everest into second place by a massive 1,000 metres (or 1 kilometre) and more. The top half of the mountain pokes out of the sea as a heavenly Hawaiian island. The rest lies hidden underwater.

3 FALSE. The Andes in South America are over 8,000 kilometres long, making them the longest mountain range on Earth. That's the same distance as from London to Peru (a handy place to start your tour of the Andes from). The awesome Andes snake all the way down the western edge of South America, through seven countries. The Rockies take second place, more than 3,000 kilometres behind.

4 TRUE. There are masses of mountains under the sea. Some stick up to form islands you can see (remember Mauna Kea?). Others aren't high enough to break the surface. A huge range of mountains runs right down the middle of the Atlantic Ocean from Iceland to Antarctica. It's over 11,000 kilometres long (that's like one and a half of the Andes). These peaks pop up when two crusty plates pull apart underwater. Red-hot, runny rock oozes up to plug the gap. It cools and goes solid, and builds freaky peaks.

5 FALSE. Mountains are much, much older than that. Take the ancient Appalchians in the USA. Give or take a few million years, they're at least 400 million years old. Imagine the dinosaurs' surprise when these freaky peaks popped up! In geological time (which is much longer than normal time – is this why your geography lessons seem to last for ever?), the Himalayas are still teenagers. Even though they're about 40 million years old.

6 FALSE. If you only count peaks over 1,000 metres high, it's true that England doesn't have any mountains. But in the whole of Britain there are a few. Ben Nevis in Scotland is 1,343 metres high. Pretty puny by freaky peak standards, but still the highest mountain in Britain. People have built a huge cairn (pile of stones) on top which adds another few metres. What d'ya mean, it's cheating?

What your teacher's score means…
If you're feeling generous, award ten points for each correct answer.
50–60 points. Top marks. Your teacher's really reached her peak. Give her a box of Rock Chocs as a prize. (She'll be too

busy picking the bits out of her teeth to give you any homework. You hope.)

30–40 points. Not bad but your teacher's probably peaked to soon. A very up-and-down performance.

20 points and below. Terrible. Your teacher needs to set her sights higher. Much higher. The only way is up from here.

Still trying to pick which peak to head for? Here's a warning. There's no time to lose. You see, mountains won't hang around for ever, however tough they seem. As soon as they're made, they start to wear out. So to find out what's getting the mountains down, cling on by your fingertips to the next cliff-hanging chapter.

FREAKY PEAK

FREAKY PEKE

SLIPPERY SLOPES

Freaky peaks look rock-solid but looks can be misleading. It's the same with some geography teachers. They might look nice and kind and reasonable but woe betide you if your homework's late. Then they turn nasty, very nasty indeed.

Mountains take millions of years to form. But no sooner has a peak reared its ugly head than the wind and the weather start wearing it down. You could say it's all downhill from then on (ha! ha!). You can spot a young mountain by its sharp, pointy peaks. As it gets older and wears out, it ends up smooth and round. Horrible geographers call this wearing down erosion. But what on Earth does it mean?

Can you spot the difference?

TABLE MOUNTAIN

MOUNTAINOUS TABLE

Table Mountain's a freaky peak in sunny South Africa. It's been worn into a shape a bit like a table by years of wind and rain. It's even got its own tablecloth (that's the name given to its cover of cloud). Whereas a table's something you eat your tea from and nothing to do with mountains. Obviously.

Erosion – the earth-shattering story

Erosion's the tricky technical term for the way the weather wears peaks away. In time it'll grind them right down into the ground. Freaky or what? Don't worry – you'd need to stick around for millions of years to see this happening. (Though some brand-new peaks might have popped up by then.) Erosion gives freaky peaks their shape. How? On weather-beaten mountains, ice is the main mover and shaker. Here's one way ice wears mountains down. What happens is this…

1. IN THE DAYTIME, WHEN THE WEATHER'S WARMER, SOME SNOW MELTS AND TRICKLES INTO CRACKS IN THE ROCKS…

2. AT NIGHT, TEMPERATURES PLUMMET, AND THE WATER FREEZES AND EXPANDS…

3. …WITH SUCH EARTH-SHATTERING FORCE IT SPLITS THE ROCK APART WITH AN INCREDIBLE, COLOSSAL…

CCRRACKK!

Sometimes seriously huge slabs of ice slip and slide down the mountainside. These are ghastly, grinding glaciers. Are you brave enough to get to know a glacier? Be warned – they're really slippery characters.

What on Earth are glaciers?

1 Glaciers are gigantic rivers of ice found on freaky peaks. But if you can't tear yourself away from the telly, why not get to grips with a slippery glacier from the comfort of your own armchair. Here's Cliff with his stay-at-home glacier guide:

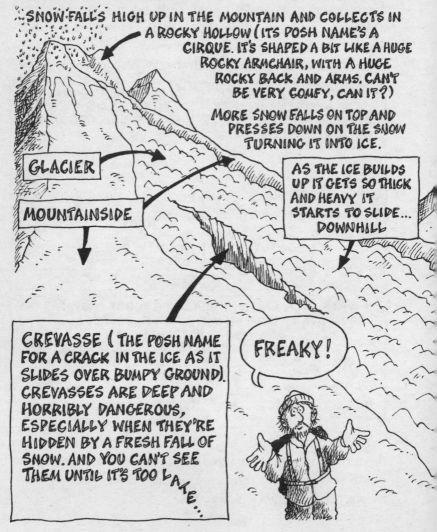

SNOW FALLS HIGH UP IN THE MOUNTAIN AND COLLECTS IN A ROCKY HOLLOW (ITS POSH NAME'S A CIRQUE. IT'S SHAPED A BIT LIKE A HUGE ROCKY ARMCHAIR, WITH A HUGE ROCKY BACK AND ARMS. CAN'T BE VERY COMFY, CAN IT?)

MORE SNOW FALLS ON TOP AND PRESSES DOWN ON THE SNOW TURNING IT INTO ICE.

GLACIER

MOUNTAINSIDE

AS THE ICE BUILDS UP IT GETS SO THICK AND HEAVY IT STARTS TO SLIDE... DOWNHILL

CREVASSE (THE POSH NAME FOR A CRACK IN THE ICE AS IT SLIDES OVER BUMPY GROUND). CREVASSES ARE DEEP AND HORRIBLY DANGEROUS, ESPECIALLY WHEN THEY'RE HIDDEN BY A FRESH FALL OF SNOW. AND YOU CAN'T SEE THEM UNTIL IT'S TOO LATE...

FREAKY!

2 Like rivers, glaciers only flow downhill. Why? What happens is that gravity drags them down. (Gravity is the force which brings things down to the ground. So if you lose your footing on a slippery slope, gravity brings you down to Earth with a bump. Ouch!) But gravity doesn't work alone. To look at, glaciers seem horribly solid but oddly, the ice inside is runny (like those yummy ice-cream lollies with gooey toffee inside … delicious). That's because it gets squashed and squeezed by all the ice on top. Then it starts to flow downhill. Glaciers usually flow slower than a snail's pace, at a slowcoach 2 metres a day. So you could easily outrun one. (You hope.)

3 You might think glistening glaciers would be nice and clear and sparkling, just like enormous ice cubes. But you'd be wrong. In fact, they're often horribly grey and grubby because of the tonnes of rock they drag along with them. The bits can be anything from boulders the size of mini mountains to minute grains of sand.

SNOUT (THE END OF THE GLACIER WHERE IT STARTS TO MELT. A BIT LIKE A RUNNY NOSE)

4 Some of the rocky bits get stuck in the ice and give the glacier its cutting edge. As it creeps along, the gritty glacier scratches and scrapes at the mountainside, like a gigantic icy scouring pad, grinding out vast U-shaped valleys. The glacier bulldozes the rest of the rock along in front of it, then dumps it at its snotty snout. The technical term for this pile of rocks is "moraine".

5 Some grinding glaciers are horribly huge. In the high-rise Himalayas, some reach a staggering 70 kilometres long and measure almost a kilometre thick. Imagine having that flowing down your street. But glaciers can shrink as well as grow. This happens when the weather turns warmer and melts the ice at the glacier's snout. Then the glacier starts to shrink in size. The Rhone glacier in the Alps started to melt in 1818. A hundred years later, it had shrunk so much that a hotel famous for its glacier-side view found itself seriously stranded.

6 Boulders aren't the only things you'll find in a ghastly glacier. In 1991, two freaked-out climbers had the shock of their lives. They stumbled across the deep-frozen body of a man poking out of a glacier in the Alps. Gruesome. They found out later that the man had died in a terrible blizzard ... more than 5,000 years before!

HE LOOKS LIKE MY OLD GEOGRAPHY TEACHER

A tale of two glaciers

Adventurous scientist Louis Agassiz (1807–1873) ended up being so gripped by ice he spent his summer holidays glacier-spotting in Switzerland. (Why not suggest this to your parents?) His sensible family didn't go with him. Most likely they'd already set off for the seaside.

Young Louis lived in Switzerland (so he didn't have far to travel to get to the awesome Alps). As a boy, he was shockingly bright and brainy. When he left school, he went off to university and got not one, but two first-class degrees, in philosophy and medicine. Swotty Louis trained to be a doctor but he gave up medicine to study ... fish. Yep, fish. Goodness knows what his teachers thought about that. It was all very fishy. But these weren't just any old fish (like the ones you get with a bag of old chips). No. These frightful fish were dead and had been for a very long time. (Imagine the deadly pong. Phwoar!) In fact, they'd been dead for so long they'd turned into fishy fossils.

Later, Louis became professor of natural history at the College of Neuchatel, where he could study his favourite fish to his heart's content. He also wrote several dead boring books, including one all about fossil starfish.

But what on Earth did these freaky fish have to do with glaciers? Nothing at all. You see, Louis got interested in glaciers by accident at a talk given by his old geography teacher. From then on, glaciers had him hooked (now he knew what a fish felt like) and he made some thrilling discoveries. Anyway, here's how he might have reported his finds in his postcards home (if he'd had time to write any).

41

The Alps, Bex, Switzerland, 1836

Dear Everyone,

The journey was fine and I got here safely. It was good to see old Mr de Charpentier again. We unpacked our bags then headed straight for the glaciers. You remember Mr de C's idea that glaciers gouge out peaks and valleys and lug giant rocks around? (no space, have to send you 2 cards)

Mr & Mrs Agassiz
Cuckoo Gardens
Yodel way
Switzerland ..

Postcard 2 ...

Well, I thought he'd lost his marbles. But he's right. That's exactly what's happened all around us. What's more, we've seen the same features and rocks in places where it isn't icy. It's a real puzzle. But Mr de C agrees with me. There must have been ancient glaciers there. A very long time ago. Thanks for the woolly gloves. Very handy.
Love from Louis XXX

Mr & Mrs Agassiz
Cuckoo Gardens
Yodel way
Switzerland

By the way, Mr de Charpentier was Louis's old teacher. Would you fancy going on holiday with your geography teacher?

Back home, Louis was invited to talk about glaciers at the Swiss Society of Natural Sciences. But his ideas met a very icy reception. One sniffy scientist even told Louis he'd be better off sticking to fish. But Louis wasn't put off. No way. He was soon heading off for the hills again...

Our Hotel!

The Unteraar Glacier, the Alps,
Switzerland 1840

Dear Everyone,
                    Here is our hotel. Ok, it's
more like a hut really. And it's horribly damp
and uncomfortable. Two walls are made of
stone. The other's a giant boulder. The roof's
another bit of rock and the door's an old blanket.
Our kitchen's a rocky ledge outside which doubles
up as our dining room. Still, who needs a fridge
when you've got a glacier? We've stuck some wine
in it to cool. Today was spent measuring how
deep the ice is. We strapped iron measuring-rods
to our backs and crawled onto the glacier.
Then we fixed the rods together and hammered
them into the ice. We finally hit rock bottom
at 300metres. Lucky I'd brought some extra
rods along. The view's fantastic.
        See you soon. Love from Louis xxx.

Mr & Mrs Agassiz
Cuckoo Gardens
Yodel Way
Switzerland

POST
OFF

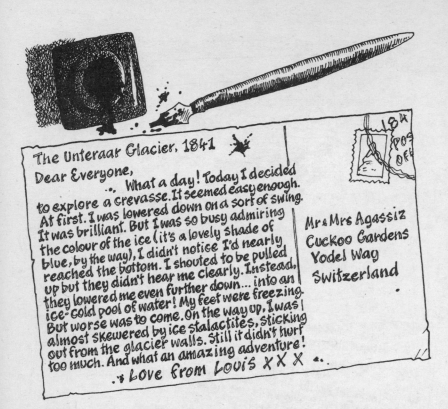

The Unteraar Glacier, 1841

Dear Everyone,

What a day! Today I decided to explore a crevasse. It seemed easy enough. At first, I was lowered down on a sort of swing. It was brilliant. But I was so busy admiring the colour of the ice (it's a lovely shade of blue, by the way), I didn't notice I'd nearly reached the bottom. I shouted to be pulled up but they didn't hear me clearly. Instead, they lowered me even further down... into an ice-cold pool of water! My feet were freezing. But worse was to come. On the way up, I was almost skewered by ice stalactites, sticking out from the glacier walls. Still it didn't hurt too much. And what an amazing adventure!

Love from Louis X X X

Mr & Mrs Agassiz
Cuckoo Gardens
Yodel Way
Switzerland

Louis's glacier-spotting holidays taught him – and us – a lot about glaciers. About 18,000 years ago, huge slices of ice covered a third of the Earth. In the Alps, the ice was so amazingly thick that only the tips of the highest peaks poked out above it. Today's glistening glaciers are all that were left when the ancient ice melted. Louis's daring discoveries soon put glaciers on the map. But Louis himself gave ice up and went off to America. He never came back. He became professor of zoology at Harvard University and turned his attention to turtles instead. But when he died, aged 66, a boulder was brought all the way from his favourite Swiss glacier to mark his grave.

Freaky peak fact file

NAME: The Alps

LOCATION: Europe (France, Italy, Switzerland, Germany and Austria)

LENGTH: 1,200 km

AGE: about 15 million years old

PEAK TYPE: Fold (see page 24)

PEAKY POINTS:

• They formed when the Eurasian Plate smashed into Africa.

• Mont Blanc in France is the highest peak at 4,807 m.

• Two small streams in the Swiss Alps mark the start of the River Rhine, one of the longest rivers in Europe.

• The longest glacier in the Alps is the Aletsch Glacier in Switzerland. It's 26 km long and the size of a small city.

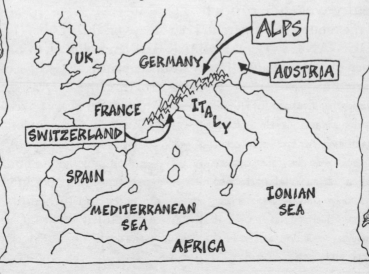

Can you spot the difference?

ROCK-CLIMBING SHEEP

SHEEPISH ROCK

Answer: The posh name for a sheepish rock is a *roche moutonée*. That's French for a sheep-shaped rock. It's the name for a hump of rock gouged out by a glacier. The ice carves out wavy grooves on its surface that look like a sheep's curly wool. (OK, so you'll need to use your imagination for this bit.) It's also the name of a groovy type of wig worn in eighteenth-century France. Must have been a very baaa-d hair day!

Peaky weather report

In the mountains, it pays to keep an eye on the weather. IF YOU WANT TO COME BACK ALIVE. Still keen to go? Then check out Cliff's freaky weather report...

Today will start off fine and clear, with clouds gathering in the afternoon. There may be the chance of a blizzard later. Expect howling winds and driving snow higher up. Or it might be calm and sunny. You just never know!

Peaky weather warning

Trouble is, freaky peak weather is horribly fickle and unpredictable. One minute, it's nice and warm and sunny, the next it's blowing up a storm. Here are four types of weather a mountain might fling at you ... IN AN HOUR.

Freezing cold. You might think the higher up you go, the warmer the weather gets. After all, you're closer to the sun. But you'd be wrong. Dead wrong. For every 100 metres you climb, it gets about 1°C colder. This is because the air high up is thin and clear. It doesn't contain any dusty specks that trap and give out heat from the sun. At the top of Mount Everest, temperatures can plummet as low as –60°C. That's as cold as the coldest day you can possibly imagine, only ten times worse. Plenty cold enough to freeze you to death.

HELLO BASECAMP, CAN YOU SEND ME UP ANOTHER 20 PAIRS OF SOCKS? OVER.

Even in summer, it's well below freezing. That's why some perishing peaks are permanently capped with snow, even if they're in warm places. Like Mount Kilimanjaro in Africa – its freaky peak is covered in glaciers all year round even though it's only a few kilometres south of the steamy equator.

AS I GET TALLER MY EARS GET COLDER

Chilly winds. Wind's a real problem up in the mountains. (No, not *that* sort of wind.) By day, the wind blows up the mountainside. At night, it blows the other way. In a matter of minutes, a gale can be gusting along at a speedy 130 kilometres per hour, as fast as a fast car. Fast enough to knock you right off your feet. Or blow you off the mountainside.

MAKE SURE YOU KEEP A FIRM GRIP

A WHAT?

What's worse, the wind makes it feel even chillier than it actually is. If the wind's blowing at 50 km/h and the temperature's –35°C, you'd freeze solid in 30 seconds. Brrr! So wrap up warm.

Lethal lightning. Lightning always takes the quickest path to the ground and hits the nearest target. So watch out if you're standing on a hill-top admiring the view: that could be you! You might end up being fried to a crisp. Or battered and bruised by rock-hard hail that falls in thunderstorms. Watch out for puffy, cauliflower-shaped clouds. They're a tell-tale sign there's a storm on the way. Or you might feel your hair standing on end (that's because of electricity in the air). Freaky. Crouch down low, until the storm blows over.

Blinding blizzards. Blizzards are horribly savage snow storms and they can strike without warning. You'll know when a blizzard hits – temperatures plummet and howling winds blast the snow straight into your mouth … so you can hardly breathe. Most of the time you can't see anything either. Blizzards can have tragic results. In fact, more climbers die from being battered by blizzards than by falling.

HORRIBLE HEALTH WARNING!

If you climb a mountain near sunrise or sunset, don't look behind you. You might see a huge, shadowy figure one step behind. Have you seen a ghost? Aaagghh! DON'T PANIC! The freaky fiend is your own shadow. Honestly. It's called the spectre of the Brocken after the Brocken Mountain in Germany where it's often seen. And there's a horribly straightforward reason for it. At sunrise and sunset, the sun is low in the sky and casts your shadow on nearby clouds. Only much, much bigger than usual. And you see a ghastly, ghostly figure. Phew!

TAP!
TAP!

One thing's for certain. Wind, snow or shine, it's tough at the top. Horribly tough and hostile. But apart from sinister shadows and sheepish rocks, surely nothing on Earth would want to live there. Would it? Oh yes, it would. Get ready for a high-rise surprise...

FREAKY NATURE

You won't find anything living right at the tops of the highest peaks. It's just too bloomin' windy and cold. But take a peek further downhill and you'll meet some horribly hardy wildlife. Peaks are perilous places to live. But, oddly enough, some plants and animals find the freezing temperatures rather bracing. They happily cope with the slippery slopes and the stormy weather. So how on Earth do they do it? The first thing to find out is which bit of the freaky peak these tough nuts call home.

WE MAY LOOK CUTE AND FLUFFY BUT IT TAKES GUTS TO SURVIVE UP HERE, YOU KNOW

Life at the top

Test your teacher's nature know-how with this tricky question: Where do you find steamy rainforests, bone-dry deserts and icy poles ... all in one place? Does he or she give up? Now show off by giving the answer – it's on a freaky peak, of course. As you go uphill, the weather changes (it gets colder the higher you go, remember?). So you start off sweltering at the bottom but break out in goose pimples near the top. Brrrr! This gives lots of different habitats (that's the posh scientific word for plant and animal homes).

Time to make friends with some freaky wildlife. Or, if you don't want to end up as a mountain lion's lunch, you could always send Cliff instead...

TREE LINE
AN IMAGINARY LINE HIGH UP ON THE MOUNTAIN. IT'S THE HIGHEST PLACE YOU'LL FIND TREES. ABOVE THIS, IT'S TOO COLD AND WINDY FOR THEM TO GROW

CONIFEROUS TREES
CONIFERS ARE TREES LIKE PINES, FIRS AND SPRUCES (AND CHRISTMAS TREES). MIND YOUR HEAD IF YOU'RE UNDERNEATH ONE. THEY'RE A BRILLIANT SHAPE FOR SHRUGGING OFF SNOW. IT SIMPLY SLIDES OFF THEIR SLANTING BRANCHES. CRASSHH!

DECIDUOUS FOREST
YOU START YOUR CLIMB IN A WARM FOREST OF SHADY OAK AND TEAK TREES (DECIDUOUS MEANS THEY LOSE THEIR LEAVES). ON OTHER PEAKS, YOU'LL FIND GRASSY PLAINS OR STEAMY RAINFOREST INSTEAD. WATCH OUT FOR HUNGRY BEARS...

TAHR (MOUNTAIN GOAT)

PIKA

SNOWCOCK

BLACK BEAR

LANGUR

TIGER

YOU START HERE

Freaky peak fact file

NAME: Himalayas

LOCATION: Asia (India, Nepal, Bhutan, Pakistan, China/Tibet, Afghanistan)

LENGTH: about 2,600 km

AGE: 30-50 million years old

PEAK TYPE: Fold (see page 24)

PEAKY POINTS:

• Their name means "abode of snow" in the ancient Indian language.

• They're the world's highest mountains with nine of the world's top ten peaks. Mount Everest's the highest.

• They're carved into shape by huge glaciers and chunks of ice.

• In the Hindu and Buddhist religions, they're believed to be the homes of the gods.

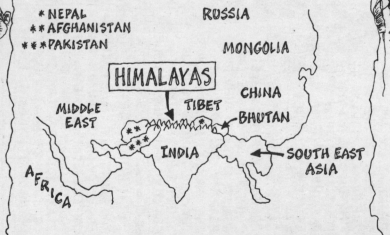

*NEPAL
**AFGHANISTAN
***PAKISTAN

RUSSIA

MONGOLIA

HIMALAYAS

TIBET

CHINA

BHUTAN

MIDDLE EAST

INDIA

SOUTH EAST ASIA

AFRICA

Peaky plant survival

You might think that faced with the cold, the wind and the dry, rocky soil, peaky plants might curl up and die. After all, without water and warmth, their cells would freeze solid and they couldn't make any food. Pretty disastrous, eh? But plenty of plucky plants grow on peaks. It's a bloomin' miracle how they do it. Luckily, they've got lots of sneaky tricks up their sleeves (sorry, leaves) to help them survive. Which of these life-saving strategies are too strange to be true?

1 The tiny shoots of the Alpine snowbell look fine and delicate. But if you picked a bunch of these for your mum, you might end up getting your fingers burned. These little beauties can give off enough heat to melt a hole in the snow. That's how they can reach the surface to bloom in spring. TRUE/FALSE?

OOH! OWW! OOH! ARGH!

2 The Rocky Mountain umbrella plant has umbrella-shaped leaves for keeping off rain and snow. It folds its leaves up neatly and puts them away when the weather turns dry and sunny. TRUE/FALSE?

3 The saussurea plant from the Himalayas is a type of daisy. But you wouldn't want to try making daisy chains with it. Its leaves are so furry and warm that bees love to snuggle up in them. And they don't like being disturbed. TRUE/FALSE?

4 Lichens grow slowly. Horribly slowly. A patch the size of a school dinner plate may be thousands of years old. This is because there may only be one day every year when it's warm enough to grow. These plants are ideal for peaks because they can eat rock. They make acids which dissolve the rocks and make them crumble. Then they send out tiny "roots" to suck up goodness from the rocks. TRUE/FALSE?

5 Some mountain trees, like willow trees, grow only a few centimetres tall. In fact, they're so small you can step right over them. They grow so low to keep out of the howling wind. Some people call them "elfin wood" because you'd have to be as titchy as an elf to count them as a wood. TRUE/FALSE?

Earth-shattering fact

Most peaky plants grow close to the ground to keep out of the wind. But not all... Some peculiar plants called lobelias and groundsels grow on the slopes of Mount Kenya in Africa. These giants can shoot up to 10 metres tall. (That's like five geography teachers standing on each other's shoulders.) But nobody knows why. In other places, they're horribly puny and small. By the way, giant groundsels are related to weedy dandelions. Imagine a dandelion that tall growing in your garden!

THESE DANDELIONS HAVE GOT TO GO

Freaky creature lifestyles

You might not think so but you have life easy. If you're cold, you just have to put on a jumper. If you're peckish, well, just raid the fridge. See? Easy, peasy. Compared to a mountain creature, at least – they have things horribly tough. But freaky creatures are fighting back. They've developed lots of cunning ways of coping with the weather and the slippery slopes (without freezing to death or falling off). Can you match each of the mountain creatures on page 58 to its horrible high-rise lifestyle?

57

1 Its dark brown colouring helps keep it warm (dark colours are better than paler colours for soaking up the sun). It lives high up on Mount Everest and eats tiny grains of pollen blown up by the wind.

2 Its thick woolly coat's so toasty warm, it sometimes gets too hot. But it also has bare patches on its legs. To cool down, it sticks its bum in the air, facing the wind. Its other horrible habit is spitting bits of smelly, chewed-up food at its enemies. (DON'T try either of these things at home.) Its cousin's a camel and it lives in the Andes.

3 It lives in the mountains of northern Japan and keeps warm in winter by taking a long, hot bath in a volcanic spring. Outside the temperature's a chilly −15°C. In the water, it's a steaming 43°C. It always tests the water first so it doesn't get its toes toasted.

4 Its hooves have sharp

MACAQUE

MOUNTAIN GOAT

SPINY LIZARD

58

edges which dig into cracks in the rocks and are hollow for sticking on to rocks, like squishy suction pads. It's brilliant at climbing and can walk along the narrowest ledges without falling off.

5 It picks up a bone from a dead goat or sheep and flies to the top of a freaky peak. Then it drops the bone on the rocks below to smash it open. It swoops down and picks at the bits of bone, especially the juicy middle.

6 It lives high on the slopes of a vile volcano in Mexico. It can cope with being frozen solid for a whole day and night, then it thaws out in the sun.

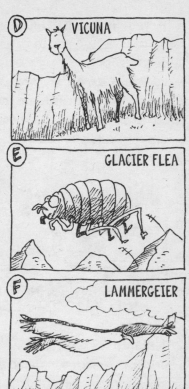

D VICUNA

E GLACIER FLEA

F LAMMERGEIER

Answers: 1 e); 2 d); 3 a); 4 b); 5 f); 6 c)

Way past your bedtime

Some peaky creatures find the best way to stay warm is by sleeping through winter and not waking up until spring. This is called hibernation. It's a good idea on a freaky peak because animals need loads of food to keep warm in cold weather. But in winter there's not much food around. So where better to be than snugly tucked up in bed? Finding it hard to stay awake? Why not spend a year with an alpine marmot?

A year in the life of an alpine marmot

Summer

You spend summer stuffing your face with food ready for the winter. Your favourite nibbles are seeds, buds and mushrooms. But you're so hungry any old mountain plants will do. You eat so much and get so fat it's a tight squeeze getting through the door of your burrow.

Autumn

You line your burrow with cosy grass and get ready for a good long kip. Actually, it's a bit of a squash - the whole family sleeps huddled close together. So you might have 14 other marmots snoring away, right in your ear. (One little sister's bad enough...) The last one in plugs up the entrance with some hay, earth and stones. You curl up into a ball and then it's off to sleep. zzzzzz.

Winter

Outside the weather's freezing cold but you're much too sleepy and snug to care. You don't even notice your breathing and pulse rates have slowed right down and your body temperature has dropped. You don't feel hungry because you live off all that extra body fat you built up in the summer. Every three to four weeks you wake up to have a poo and a wee. Good job you're too tired to notice the pong.

Spring

Wakey, wakey! Rise and shine. You've been fast asleep for SIX WHOLE MONTHS. What d'ya mean you're still sleepy? You've lost about a quarter of your body weight - say hello to the new, slim-line you! Now it's time to go out into the big, wide world ... and to spring clean your smelly burrow!

A freaky mountain mystery

Many peaky creatures are horribly shy. It's hard enough just staying alive without making friends as well. But there's one animal that's more mysterious than most. In fact, it's a mystery if it exists at all. What on Earth could this freaky beast be? Brace yourself. You're about to find out…

For centuries, people in the Himalayas have told stories of a huge, shaggy-haired creature called a yeti roaming the mountains. Is it a man? Is it an ape? Nobody knows. You see, no one has ever got close enough to a yeti to find out for sure. And there aren't any yetis in wildlife parks or zoos for horrible scientists to study. So we decided to send our own expedition to track down a real-live yeti. Plenty of other expeditions had tried and failed. Would we be the first to come face-to-face with this elusive beast? But first we needed a volunteer. Someone incredibly brave and intrepid. Someone who didn't feel the cold. Someone just like Cliff, the climber...

Here's Cliff's report and it makes riveting reading. Go on, take a peek ... if you dare.

The Case of the Missing YETI

You know me, I love a good mountain. That's why I took this job. It seemed right up my street (or should that be peak, ha! ha!). Besides, I'd seen these detective dudes on the telly and it looked like a cinch. That was my first big mistake. Anyway, my first job was to interview the suspect. It was easier said than done. I decided to hit the top secret files and find out exactly what I was up against.

1 The suspect

NAME: Yeti
DESCRIPTION:

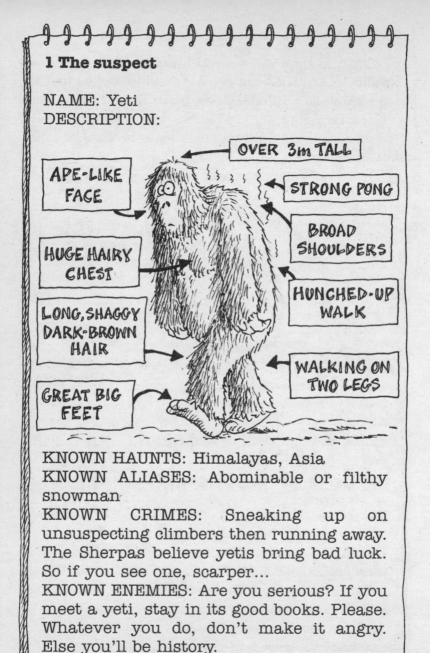

OVER 3m TALL

APE-LIKE FACE

STRONG PONG

BROAD SHOULDERS

HUGE HAIRY CHEST

HUNCHED-UP WALK

LONG, SHAGGY DARK-BROWN HAIR

WALKING ON TWO LEGS

GREAT BIG FEET

KNOWN HAUNTS: Himalayas, Asia
KNOWN ALIASES: Abominable or filthy snowman
KNOWN CRIMES: Sneaking up on unsuspecting climbers then running away. The Sherpas believe yetis bring bad luck. So if you see one, scarper...
KNOWN ENEMIES: Are you serious? If you meet a yeti, stay in its good books. Please. Whatever you do, don't make it angry. Else you'll be history.

2 Video diary from the scene of the crime

Cunningly disguised as a, er, yeti, I headed for the Himalayas to investigate the scene of the crime. First stop was Mount Annapurna where several yetis have been spotted in recent years. One was seen (and heard) by two British climbers as they were setting up their camp. They watched it wander about for ten minutes or so before it vanished. Apparently.

10:22   REC●

Well, things have started off well, I must say. I'd only been here for a few hours when I stumbled across a steaming pile of dung. Actually I put my foot straight in it. I've taken a sample to study later (the things we geographers have to do) but I'm pretty certain it's yeti poo. And on one of my late night walks (more later), I spotted some footprints in the snow. They're not mine and there's no one else around. Very suspicious. So who on Earth do they belong to?

13:15

RECO

A few days later...

The trail's gone cold. I've been here for over a week now and I still haven't seen an actual yeti in the flesh. Trouble is, yetis are said to be nocturnal (they only come out at night). So they're horribly hard to see in the dark.

09:32

RECO

A few more days later…

What's more, someone or something's pinched the last of the sausages I was saving for my tea. One thing's for sure, there aren't any yetis in this neck of the woods. I'm outta here.

15:59   BAT. LOW   RECO

3 The evidence

So far, my mission hadn't been a great success. I was the first to admit it. There was only one thing to do — I decided to head home and hit the files again. (Goodbye, yeti suit. Hoorah!) It was time to get to grips with the evidence. Fortunately, other yeti hunters have been luckier than me. So what had they found out so far?

1 Eyewitness accounts. There have been hundreds of sightings of a yeti. And several serious scientific expeditions have set off to catch one and bring it back. In the 1980s, a Canadian climber, Robert Hutchinson, launched Yeti '88, the most ambitious yeti hunt ever.

He wanted to find a yeti and collect some yeti poo (smelly but brilliant scientific evidence, as I found out). He spent five months following yeti tracks but sadly the yeti

that made them kept giving him the slip. I know just how he felt.

2 Frozen footprints. In 1951, top British explorer, Eric Shipton, snapped a trail of giant footprints high up on Mount Everest. Each foot had three small toes and

one much bigger toe. No human could have made them. The only creature the feet might fit was an orang utan (but orang utans live thousands of kilometres away) ... or a yeti.

3 Sacred scalps. One expedition claimed to have seen an actual scalp from a yeti. It was long and cone-shaped and covered in short, reddish hair. It was kept in a Buddhist monastery near Mount Everest. The monks worshipped the scalp as a sacred relic (that's a precious holy object). The scalp was taken back to London and examined under a

microscope. Sadly, the scientists said it wasn't a yeti's but belonged to a boring mountain goat. But even scientists can be wrong sometimes, can't they?

4 The verdict

So the evidence was mounting up. But what would the final verdict be? Did yetis exist? Or was the whole thing a load of old yeti poo? Anyway, I'd done my bit. I'd even kind of enjoyed it. But now it was time to hand the whole freaky case over to the experts...

No, yetis don't exist. Don't be silly. The photos and footprints must be fakes. All you need is a pair of yeti-print boots and the rest is easy. Besides, the thin mountain air plays terrible tricks on you. You might think you've seen something spooky but it's all in the mind. But if there is something there, and I only say maybe, my guess is it's a bear or a (large-ish) monkey. (Which also explains all that poo.)

YETI? SPAGHETTI!

Of course yetis exist. Everyone knows that. OK so scientists haven't caught one yet but it's just a matter of time. They're either a brand-new giant ape yeti, sorry, yet, to be discovered by science. Or a descendant of ancient horrible humans who've been hiding in the mountains for years and years. Who knows, it could be a long-lost relation?

GO GET A YETI

You might think yetis are about as freaky and far out as it gets. But you'd be wrong. Horribly wrong. There are some far stranger creatures lurking on the mountainside. The question is, are you brave enough to meet them? Turn the page quietly in case you disturb them...

PEAKS and PEOPLE

If you were looking for somewhere to live, what would it be like? Hot and sunny? Near the sea? Nowhere near a freaky peak? Surely no one would want to live there? Well, you're wrong. Despite the horribly harsh conditions, an amazing 500 million people – that's about a tenth of the world's population – live on mountains. So how on Earth do these peaky people cope with their high-rise lifestyle?

Peaky people

The Quechua Indians live high up in the Andes mountains in South America. They mostly live by farming crops, such as potatoes, barley and maize. They also keep cattle, sheep, chickens and ... llamas. If you're going to live on a mountain, a llama's a horribly useful animal to have. They're brilliant for riding and carrying heavy loads, and you can weave their super-soft wool into toasty warm clothes. By the way, llamas are close cousins of camels, except they don't have humps.

But if you're thinking of paying a Quechua village a visit, be warned. As you go higher, the thin mountain air might leave you feeling dizzy and gasping for breath. That's why the hardy Quechua have slightly bigger hearts and lungs than most people to carry more oxygen in their blood.

They've also found ways of coping with the freezing mountain temperatures: while you're pulling on another pair of thick, llama-wool socks, they'll happily walk barefoot in the snow. That's because their feet have extra blood vessels which stop them getting cold, so they're less likely to get frostbite. An amazing feet, sorry, feat.

Freaky peak fact file

NAME: The Andes

LOCATION: South America (Argentina, Chile, Bolivia, Peru, Ecuador, Columbia, Venezuela)

LENGTH: 7,250 km

AGE: 138–165 million years old

PEAK TYPE: Fold (see page 24)

PEAKY POINTS:

• They're the longest mountain range in the world

• Their highest peak is Aconcagua (6,960 m). This freaky peak's name means "Guard of Stone".

• They formed when the Pacific Ocean plate plunged under South America.

• They're so high they block winds and rain clouds. So it rains on the east side but on the west lies dusty desert.

Peaky perks

Living in the mountains is horribly hard and many peaky people are very poor and struggle to survive. That's why many are now leaving the mountains behind to try their luck in big towns and cities.

But it isn't all doom and gloom. Even the freakiest peaks have their uses. Here are four freaky things you might not expect to find up a perilous peak:

1 Wonderful water. Forget banana milkshakes or cans of fizzy pop, if you're thirsty you can't beat a glass of water. In fact, wonderful water's vital for keeping you alive. Without it, you'd be dead in days. Most of our drinking water comes from raging rivers. But do you know where these rivers start? Up freaky peaks, of course. Some of the biggest rivers on Earth start off as bubbling mountain streams. Some leak from lofty hillside lakes. Others glug from the ends of icy glaciers.

Believe it or not, about half of all the world's drinking water comes from these freaky flows.

2 Shocking electricity. But water's not just for drinking. You can also make electricity from it. (Think about that next time you switch on your computer.) If you live near a mountain, here's what might be happening…

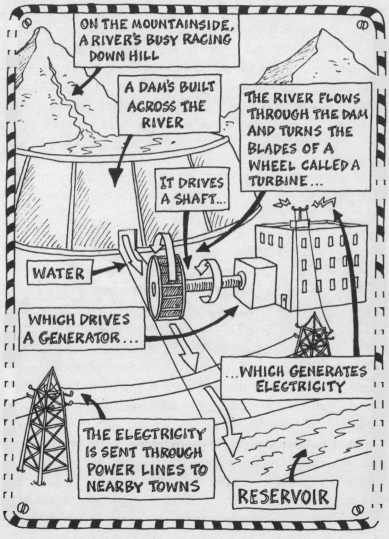

ON THE MOUNTAINSIDE, A RIVER'S BUSY RACING DOWN HILL

A DAM'S BUILT ACROSS THE RIVER

THE RIVER FLOWS THROUGH THE DAM AND TURNS THE BLADES OF A WHEEL CALLED A TURBINE…

IT DRIVES A SHAFT…

WATER

WHICH DRIVES A GENERATOR…

…WHICH GENERATES ELECTRICITY

THE ELECTRICITY IS SENT THROUGH POWER LINES TO NEARBY TOWNS

RESERVOIR

3 Fragile fields. Many peaky people make their living by farming. But it's a horribly hard and back-breaking job. You won't find a nice, flat green field to plant crops in. The soil's much too poor and dusty, and the slope's too slippery and steep. So what on Earth do farmers do? Sherpa farmers in Nepal cut huge, flat steps into the hillside and use them as fields. Then they build walls around them to hold the soil and water in. Clever, eh? On the steps, they grow crops such as potatoes, rice, wheat, barley and apricots. They also keep animals like sheep, goats and cattle. In winter, they keep the animals indoors or in the warmer valleys. In summer, they drive them up the mountain to graze on the lush, green pasture high up.

ER... IT'S GETTING A BIT NIPPY UP HERE

4 Glittering gold. One thing you'll find plenty of up a freaky peak is rock. Piles and piles of the stuff. But scratch the surface and you might be surprised. Some mountain rocks are rich in gold, silver, copper, tin and other precious metals. (Not to mention gorgeous gemstones such as rubies and emeralds.) And mining these metals is very big business. But gold-digging's horribly dicey. You might strike lucky or you might not. And it takes time to dig a gold mine in a mountain because some mines are thousands of metres deep.

But if you're fed up with paltry pocket money, why not get rich quick and go panning for gold?

What you need:
- a large sieve or pan
- a mountain stream
- a touchstone (a dark rock)
- bags of patience

What you do:

a) Dip your sieve into the stream and fill it with sand and water.

b) Carefully swirl your sieve round to swill the sand and water away.

c) Any gold will settle in the bottom of your sieve as flakes, grains or nuggets.

d) To see if your gold's real, scratch it with your touchstone. If it leaves a yellow streak ... congratulations! You've struck lucky. (If it doesn't, more fool you. It's probably a rock called pyrite or "fool's gold".)

Freaky peak transport

OK, so your arms ache from all that sieving but at least you're filthy rich. The question is, what on Earth are you going to spend your gold on? If you're living on a far-out peak, you can't just pop along to the shops. They're most likely miles and miles away. (On the bright side, this could make getting to school pretty tricky. Hoorah!) So how do peaky people get from A to B? If you're planning a freaky journey, check out the timetable below. You don't want to miss the bus, do you? There may not be another one along for weeks and weeks. Here's Cliff to see you off.

PEAKY TRANSPORT TIMETABLE

1 Walking tours

Feeling fit? Put your best foot forward and walk. That's how most peaky people get about. The Sherpa people are so super-fit and hardy, they're hired to lug climbers' bags up the mountainside. (Talk about cheating!) The Sherpas live high up in the Himalayas in Nepal, especially around Mount Everest. They can walk for hours and hours, using an even, padding stride that's very energy-efficient. And the Sherpas know all the best places to stop for a rest. By the way, they believe that the peaks are home to the mountain gods. So they always say a prayer or two for a safe journey before setting off.

I WONDER IF HE COULD CARRY ME AS WELL!

- Journey time: Depends how fast you walk.
- Risk of breakdown: Depends how fit you're feeling.

HORRIBLE HEALTH WARNING

Never mess with mountain gods. They've got really terrible tempers. A legend tells of a greedy chief who sent his army up Mount Kilimanjaro to collect the shimmering silver on top. (OK, so you know it's a glacier but he'd never even heard of such a thing.) Only one warrior lived to tell the freaky tale. He said the gods killed the men, and made their fingers and toes drop off (he hadn't heard of frostbite either). As for the silver? Well, it turned to water in their hands. Of course.

2 Yak-back riding

Hitch a lift on a yak for hikes above 6,000 metres. With their long, shaggy coats, these freaky creatures don't feel the cold. And they'll take the steepest slopes and fastest rivers in their stride. A serious expedition up Everest uses 60 yaks to carry its gear. What's more, you can use yak's milk for making butter and yoghurt, the hide for boots, and the hair for handy ropes. You can even eat yaks, if you're desperate. Expecting a letter? Watch out for the yak-back post.

I SEEM TO BE YAK-TO-FRONT!

- Journey time: Yak pace is about the same as walking pace, even with you on its back.
- Risk of breakdown: Very low. Yaks are terrifically tough. But if your yak plays up, try pinching its nose with your thumb and middle finger. Then hold on tight!

3 Take the tunnel

For an easy ride, head for a tunnel. They carry roads and railways through mountainsides. (Otherwise you'd just have to go the long way round!) There are plenty of tunnels around the world, especially in the Alps. The first one ever was the Mont Cenis tunnel between Italy and France built in 1857. It was 13 kilometres long. First, the tunnellers had to blast their way through the solid rock using tonnes of dynamite. Then they dug and drilled out the loose rock. It was stuffy, airless and the rocks got horribly hot. No wonder the tunnel took 13 long years to finish.

I'LL BE GLAD TO SEE THE LIGHT AT THE END OF THIS TUNNEL

- Journey time: About five minutes to drive straight through the Mont Cenis tunnel to get from Italy to France.
- Risk of breakdown: Quite low. Today's tunnels are massively strong but there's still a risk of fatal fires.

4 Hit the high road

If you get car-sick on the way to school, you might like to skip the next bit. Building a road up a mountainside is an amazing engineering feat. You can't just build a nice straight road up and down – the slope's too steep for that. So engineers have to build extra-long, extra-twisty roads with loads of horribly scary "hairpin" bends. (They're called hairpins because they look like those wiggly wire things that keep your granny's hair in place.) Talk about going round the bend. Where's that sick bag. . .?

THIS IS DRIVING ME ROUND THE BEND!

- Journey time: Take it slowly. Very slowly. And watch out for rockfalls and avalanches.
- Risk of breakdown: Check your brakes before you set out. And don't get too close to the edge.

5 Go by train

Let the train take the strain. But get ready for a rocky ride. Like roads, railways can't go straight up and down. They have to snake up slopes in giant loops and zig-zags. On very steep slopes, an extra wheel on the train fits into an extra bit of track to stop the train slipping backwards. If you're feeling brave, hop on the Trans-Andean mountain railway in Chile. In places, the train chugs along at over 4,500 metres. It'll take your breath away. Passengers are given oxygen to stop them feeling queasy in the thin mountain air. Don't forget to pack a picnic and wrap up warm — there's no food or heating on board.

- **Journey time:** The journey on the Trans-Andean should take about 30 hours but allow a couple of days. It never leaves or arrives on time.
- **Risk of breakdown:** Quite high. Add another day on to your journey time.

And finally…

While you're recovering from your hair-raising journey, here's some good news: freaky peak living is good for your health. It's official. In the Caucasus Mountains, people regularly live to 100 years old. Even your geography teacher isn't that ancient. They put it down to the bracing mountain air and … yoghurt. Yes, yoghurt. A good, big bowlful every day. So stock up the fridge and get slurping…

CLIMB EVERY MOUNTAIN

Each year, thousands of horribly hardy humans climb up freaky peaks. FOR FUN! If you ask them why, they'll probably look rather sheepish and mutter about good exercise and the stunning views. Or they'll say it's because the mountains are there (remember the stair experiment?). A barmy but brilliant excuse. Why not try it next time your mum catches you scoffing the last of the choccy chip ice-cream? So are these crazy climbers mad, bad or hopelessly lost? Read on and find out. You'll be gripped*.

> * Apart from meaning horribly excited, "gripped" is also a term climbers use. It means being so scared stiff you can't move a single muscle. You can't climb up. You can't climb down. You can only cling on for dear life. Don't say you weren't warned...

Reaching for the top

Impress your teacher and freak out your friends with some fascinating facts about mad mountaineers. That way you can climb every mountain without leaving your armchair.

The first person known to climb a mountain simply for the thrill of getting to the top was dashing French captain, Antoine de Ville. In June 1492, King Charles VIII ordered him to lead a group of climbers to the top of Mont Aiguille, a 2,097-metre peak in the Alps. (Mont Aiguille's French for Needle

Mountain. No wonder when you see its nasty needle-sharp peak. Ouch!) In those days it paid to keep the king happy. Otherwise it might be your head on the chopping block. Anyway, daring de Ville clambered up Needle Mountain on a series of ladders and was so impressed by the stunning views, he stayed on the summit for three whole days. (He also thought it made him look ever so important. What a show-off!)

HE'S REALLY BEGINNING TO NEEDLE ME

But climbing mountains for fun was horribly slow to catch on. Local people especially kept freaky peaks at arm's length. The further away, the better. They thought they were full of witches and demons. They might climb a mountain to get from A to B. But sightseeing was out. It wasn't until 1760, almost 300 years after Antoine's lofty ascent, that anyone took mountain climbing seriously. Then top Swiss geographer, Horace Bénédict de Saussure, offered a cash prize to the first person to climb mighty Mont Blanc, the highest peak in Europe. Even then, it took 26 long years for a willing victim, sorry, volunteer to come forward…

Melting moments on Mont Blanc
Dr Michel-Gabriel Paccard from Chamonix, France, had spent years gawping at Mont Blanc through his telescope. That freaky peak had him hooked. He tried to climb it a couple of times but couldn't quite reach the top. But he wasn't about to give up now. Oh, no. Besides, Horace's dosh

would come in handy. So, at 4.30 a.m. on 8 August 1786, plucky Dr Paccard set off. With him, he took Jacques Balmat, a local crystal hunter, who knew the mountain like the back of his hand. (Except for the very top bit, of course.) As for climbing kit? Well, between them, they had a walking stick each, some bread, meat and a threadbare blanket. Woe betide them if a blizzard struck.

From the start, the going was horribly hard. The trouble was, the weather was warm for the time of year and the ice kept melting beneath them. The only way to cross the colossal crevasses was to fall flat on their faces and wriggle over. To make matters worse, it was horribly windy. They stopped for lunch at 3,350 metres (making sandwiches was out – the meat had frozen solid by this time).

Then they continued their hair-raising climb. But by this time battered Balmat had had enough. He refused to go any further. Somehow, Paccard persuaded him to carry on. Before them loomed a steep icy slope. Plucky Paccard led the way, chipping steps with his ice axe.

86

Finally, at 6.32 p.m., our two horrible heroes reached the summit. It had taken them 14 long, weary hours. Both men were freezing cold, worn out and suffering from frostbite and snow blindness. But there was no time to rest. There was nowhere to camp on the mountain top so they had to climb straight back down. They reached home at 8 a.m. the following morning and went straight to bed.

But they'd earned their place in the history books ... and de Saussure's prize.

Earth-shattering fact
Thank your lucky stars you weren't on William Green's expedition up Mount Cook in 1882. He and two guides almost reached the summit when terrible weather forced them back. But on the way down, darkness fell. They were stuck. So they spent the night perched on a tiny ledge, clinging on for dear life. If they'd fallen asleep, they'd have dropped straight off. Simple as that. To stay awake, they sucked sweets and sang hymns. (Luckily, William was a vicar so he knew all the words.)

More mountains to climb

After the thrilling conquest of Mont Blanc, mountaineering never looked back. Climbing became all the rage. Anyone who was anyone joined a climbing club and set off in search of adventure. Peak after peak in the Alps was climbed, one after the other. Then dare-devil climbers set their sights further afield – South America, Africa and Asia. But what about the freakiest mountains of all, the mighty Himalayas? The meanest, moodiest mountains on Earth. Who would reach the top of the world first? The race was on…

EXCUSE ME, COMING THROUGH

I DO BEG YOUR PARDON

MAKE WAY THERE

Mystery on the mountain

In 1924, a British expedition of 300 climbers and porters set out to climb Mount Everest. After two years of planning, waiting and organizing, hopes were high. Their route lay up the north side of the mountain in Tibet. For years, Tibet had been out of bounds to foreigners. But in the 1920s, it began to allow foreign climbers in. They seized their chance. Among them was George Leigh Mallory, perhaps the finest and most famous mountaineer of his day. (And the first person to say: "Because it was there.") He'd already been to Everest twice and failed to reach the top. This time he was sure he'd make it. Or die in the attempt. Nobody dared to doubt him. If Mallory couldn't do it, no one could.

Here's how the newspapers of the time might have reported what happened…

The Daily Globe
Mount Everest, Tibet

PLUCKY CLIMBERS PERISH ON WORLD'S HIGHEST PEAK

Climbers George Leigh Mallory and Andrew Irvine were feared dead last night, having gone missing on Mount Everest. It is thought that the plucky pair may have plummeted to their deaths, only a few hundred metres from the summit of the world's highest peak.

MALLORY AND IRVINE

The last person to see the two men alive was fellow-climber Noel Odell. He had been setting up camp lower down, ready for Mallory and Irvine's return. Looking up, he spied the two men through a rare break in the clouds, moving well and going strong. It was 12.50 p.m. on 8 June. The men were just 245 metres from the summit.

SO NEAR...

"My eyes became fixed on one tiny black spot silhouetted on a small snow crest beneath a rock step in the ridge," Odell told our reporter. "The black spot moved. Another black spot became apparent and moved up the snow to join the other on the crest. The first then approached the great rock step and shortly emerged on top.

The second did likewise. Then the whole fascinating vision was enveloped in cloud once more."

Mallory and Irvine were never seen again. Mallory, 37, a schoolmaster, had been climbing since his schooldays. Friends and colleagues alike describe him as daring, dashing and one of the greatest climbers of his age. He leaves behind a wife, Ruth, and three young children.

Andrew "Sandy" Irvine, 22, was a promising student at Oxford University. A brilliant sportsman, he and Mallory had become good friends.

Today, tributes poured in to these two brave men, including this one from King George V of England: "They will ever be remembered as fine examples of mountaineers," he said, "ready to risk their lives for their companions and to face dangers on behalf of science and discovery."

A TOP PAIR

We may never know if they made it to the top, or died in the trying.

An icy grave

In March 1999, 75 years after Mallory's death, an American expedition made an astonishing discovery. They were hoping to find Irvine's body. From an ice axe found in 1933 and eyewitness accounts, they thought they knew where he lay. A body was spotted in the snow, lying face down in its icy grave. Was it Irvine? It must be. But the carefully stitched name tags on the tattered clothes told a different story. "G. Mallory", they read. George Mallory. Unbelievably, they had found their hero. With great respect, the climbers buried Mallory's body where it lay, on the mountain he loved.

But the mystery remained. Had Mallory and Irvine made it to the top, 29 years before Tenzing and Hillary? Or had they perished on their way to the summit? Who better to ask than two clued-up climbers...

> Yes. Noel Odell had excellent eyesight and when he spotted them, they were half-way there. And they had plenty of oxygen left. Besides, it was Mallory's last expedition. He wanted to spend more time at home. It was his life's ambition to climb Mount Everest. For him, it was all or nothing. If only Irvine's camera could be found. A photo of the two men on top of Everest would prove it once and for all.

> No. They must have turned back before the summit and died on the way down. They'd never have made it up the Second Step. It's a sheer wall of rock 30 metres tall. Mountaineers today can only get up it on ladders. Also, they'd only got a few hours of daylight left and they'd left their torches behind. Even so, it's incredible they got as high as they did. Higher than anyone had climbed before.

Hmm. Even the experts can't agree. Perhaps this is a mystery that'll never be solved. What do you think?

Freaky peak photo album

Meanwhile, Cliff's been busy with his camera, taking shots of other famous mountaineers. Yes, I know other people's holiday snaps can be horribly boring. But this freaky photo album will have you gripped with excitement. Not convinced? Look on the bright side. It's got to be better than geography homework.

William got into freaky peaks by accident. He was actually looking for goats. He trained as a vet then went to India to set up a shawl-making factory. And the wool for the shawls came from, yes, you've guessed it, goats which lived in the Himalayan mountains. So, in 1812, woolly-headed William set off, disguised as a holy man. (At that time, outsiders weren't very welcome. Without his disguise, he'd have been killed.) Despite being kidnapped and clapped in jail, William finally got his goats. And became the first outsider to explore the mountains. But it was very slow going – the journey took six long years. Still, there was no point bleating about it.

Henriette was the first woman to climb Mont Blanc in 1838. (On her own two feet: in 1808, a young girl was carried to the top to sell food to hungry climbers.) In those days, climbing wasn't considered particularly ladylike and girls had to wear long, tweed skirts. Very respectable but not very practical. (Makes your school uniform look really cool.) But rebellious Henriette cheated and wore a pair of brightly checked trousers under hers. A carrier pigeon brought news of her climb down from the top. Henriette herself toasted her triumph with a glass of ice-cold champagne. Cheers!

Henriette d'Angeville

Photos

Intrepid Isabella started travelling on doctor's orders. A long journey would do her good, he said. Her family wanted her to get married and settle down but that was much too boring for her. Instead, she set off, alone, for Colorado, USA, to climb the Rocky Mountains. There she fell in love with a no-good bandit called Mountain Jim. Tragically, Jim was later shot dead in a gun fight. In between trips, Isabella wrote best-selling books about her travels. And in case she had any time to spare, she always took her knitting along. At least she never ran out of warm, woolly gloves.

Freaky peak fact file

NAME: The Rocky Mountains (Rockies, for short)
LOCATION: North America (Canada and the USA)
LENGTH: 4,800 km
AGE: about 80 million years old
PEAK TYPE: Fold (see page 24)
PEAKY POINTS:

- The highest peak is Mount Elbert in Colorado at 4,399 m.
- Some of North America's biggest rivers start flowing in the Rockies. They include the Missouri, Rio Grande, Columbia and Colorado, to name a few.
- Many slopes are covered in massive forests of sequoia and redwood trees, the tallest trees in the world. They're cut down for their valuable timber.
- The chinook's a famous local wind that blows in winter. It brings a spell of hot, dry weather, melting the snow. That's why it's nicknamed "snow eater".

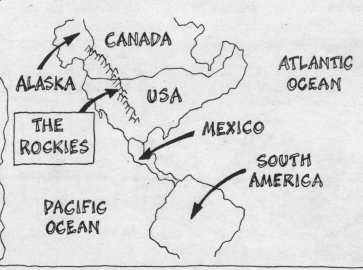

CANADA

ALASKA

USA

ATLANTIC OCEAN

THE ROCKIES

MEXICO

SOUTH AMERICA

PACIFIC OCEAN

This is me with Edward Whymper, the first man up the Matterhorn. (Okay, so I'm making the first bit up.) Edward started out as an artist but he gave it up as a job for whymps, sorry, wimps. He climbed this freaky peak on 14 July 1865, beating a team of Italians. (Actually, Edward spotted them below and chucked rocks at them to scare them off.) On the way down, Edward's team was roped together for safety. Then tragedy struck when one man slipped, dragging three others to their deaths. Whymper only survived because the rope broke. It was a very lucky escape.

A life of fetching sticks and chewing slippers was not for this plucky pooch. Between 1868 and 1876, Tschingel the beagle climbed more than 50 major Alpine peaks with her owner, American William Coolidge. And that's a doggy record. To top it all, in 1875, she became the first dog to climb Mont Blanc. On several occasions, Tschingel nearly plunged to her death but was caught by the rope threaded through her collar. But she refused to wear the leather boots doting William had made for her. Woof! Woof!

Reinhold Messner born 1944

Italian climber, Reinhold Messner, is probably the greatest modern-day mountaineer. By the age of 13, he'd already climbed many awesome Alpine peaks. Between 1970 and 1986, he became the first person to climb all 14 of the world's highest peaks (the ones more than 8,000 metres tall). What's more, he was also the first to climb Mount Everest without using oxygen and the first to climb it solo (without ropes or guides). What a guy!

What goes up, must come down

You know the saying "What goes up, must come down"? Well, generally speaking it's true. Picture the scene … you've dragged yourself up your freaky peak, you've soaked in the scenery and it's time to head down. Easier said than done. Here are five way-out ways to reach rock bottom. Can you tell which ones are too risky to be real?

1. SKIING…
2. HANG-GLIDING…
3. CANOEING…
4. ZIP WIRING…
5. GLISSADING…

Answers: Believe it or not, all of these are true. What's more, they've all been tried and tested…

1 Every year, thousands of people take to the hills to experience the thrills and spills of skiing. They catch the lift up, then ski back down. For fun, apparently. But downhill skiing's a serious sport – you'd have to be seriously barmy to do it. The world's top skiers hurtle downhill at staggering speeds of almost 250 kilometres per hour. That's as fast as a high-speed train. Whoosh!

2 In the 1980s, two French climbers, Boivin and Marchal, came down from the summit of Mount Aconcagua, not on foot … but by hang-glider! They landed about half-way down the mountain, having soared in the air for 20 minutes. Lucky they didn't get carried away.

LOOK! I'M HANG-HANG-GLIDING!

3 In 1976, two British canoeists, Mike Jones and Mike Hopkinson, canoed down the Dudh Kosi River on Mount Everest. This high-rise river flows from an icy lake more than 5,000 metres up on the Khumbu Icefall. Blocks of ice the size of houses regularly break off this ghastly glacier and crash into the river below.

4 Get this. A person slides down a rope from the top of a cliff … by his or her ankle. Or sitting on a bicycle. Unbelievably some freaky people do this for a thrill. WARNING: this is a horribly dangerous thing to do. Never, ever try it.

5 Glissading comes from a French word for sliding. It means slipping and sliding down a steep icy slope on your feet … or on your bum. The fastest descent of Mount Everest was made in 1986. Two climbers glissaded down 2,500 metres on their bottoms. When they wanted to stop, they used their ice axes as brakes. Their slide took 3.5 hours. Painful!

Could you be a top mountaineer? Are you daring enough to climb Mount Everest? If you like living on the edge, hurry into the next chapter for the adventure of a lifetime. But if all this excitement's left you exhausted, don't freak out. If your teacher's so keen on freaky peak field trips, why not send her instead?

Freaky peaks are perilous places to be. But if your teacher's dead set on getting to the top, has she really got what it takes to be a top mountaineer? Is she fighting fit? Cool in a crisis? Does she have a good head for heights? Is she breath-takingly brave and horribly hardy? Where she's going, she'll need to be. Mountaineering's not for the faint-hearted. Is she still keen to go? Is she stark staring bonkers? Luckily she'll have Cliff to show her the ropes...

Are you brave enough to climb Mount Everest?

What you need:
- a very large mountain
- lots of posh climbing clothes

If you're climbing a freaky peak, you need to dress for the part. There's no point setting off up Mount Everest in jeans and a T-shirt, however cool you think you look. You need clothes that'll protect you from the cold and wind, otherwise you'll freeze to death. Don't worry, there's lots of trendy kit around to keep you snug as a bug. Look over the page to see me modelling the latest red-hot look in groovy climbing gear. It's what every modern mountaineer's wearing...

COOL CLIMBERS 1: MODERN MOUNTAINEER

CLIMBING SUIT:
A ONE-PIECE SUIT FILLED WITH DOWN (A BIT LIKE A DUVET WITH ARMS AND LEGS). IT'S WINDPROOF, WATERPROOF AND WELL-INSULATED. (TO TRAP WARMTH NEXT TO YOUR BODY). IT'S ALSO "BREATHABLE" (TO LET SWEAT ESCAPE). IT'S BEST TO WEAR LAYERS UNDERNEATH SO YOU CAN TAKE THEM OFF IF YOU GET TOO HOT (YES IT HAPPENS).

HOOD:
TO KEEP OUT THE WIND AND SNOW. BIG ENOUGH TO FIT A CRASH HELMET UNDERNEATH.

HEADTORCH:
YOU DON'T WANT TO LOSE YOUR WAY IN THE DARK.

WARM FLEECY HAT OR BALACLAVA:
IF IT'S VERY COLD, WEAR IT UNDER YOUR HELMET.

GLACIER GOGGLES:
TO PROTECT YOUR EYES FROM GLARE.

THERMAL T-SHIRT AND THERMAL UNDERWEAR

THIN FLEECE:
FLEECE IS A FLUFFY FABRIC. IT'S LIGHT, WARM AND QUICK TO DRY.

SKI POLES:
HANDY FOR KEEPING YOUR BALANCE.

ICE AXE: FOR CUTTING STEPS IN SNOW AND STOPPING YOUR-SELF IF YOU START SLIDING. MADE OF LIGHTWEIGHT STEEL.

RUCKSACK:
FOR CARRYING SPARE SUPPLIES. MADE OF TOUGH NYLON.

GLOVES:
BEST TAKE TWO PAIRS: A THIN THERMAL PAIR AND A PAIR OF DOWN MITTENS.

THICK SOCKS:
MADE FROM WOOL AND NYLON.

OXYGEN SUPPLY:
IN HANDY LIGHTWEIGHT BOTTLES.

STURDY BOOTS:
THEY'RE MADE FROM PLASTIC WITH STIFF SOLES FOR KICKING STEPS IN THE SNOW AND GRIPPING THE GROUND. LIGHT, WARM AND WATERPROOF.

CRAMPONS:
METAL SPIKES STRAPPED TO THE SOLES OF YOUR BOOTS TO GRIP THE ICE AND SNOW.

SUNSCREEN AND LIP SALVE:
THE SUN CAN BE VERY STRONG.

GAITERS:
COVERS YOU CLIP OVER THE TOP OF YOUR BOOTS TO KEEP OUT STONES AND WATER.

Just so you realize how lucky you are, here's what a climber would have worn in the 1920s (in George Mallory's day). Imagine climbing Mount Everest in this lot…

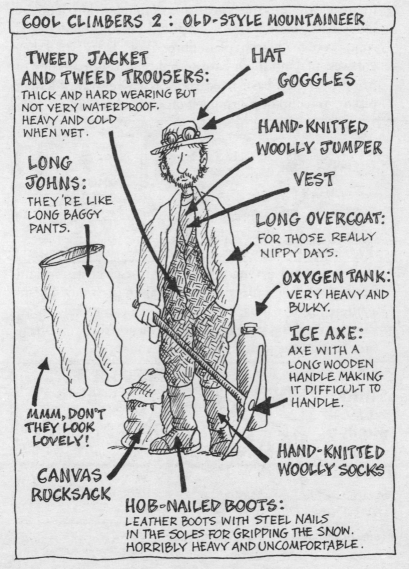

COOL CLIMBERS 2 : OLD-STYLE MOUNTAINEER

HAT

GOGGLES

TWEED JACKET AND TWEED TROUSERS:
THICK AND HARD WEARING BUT NOT VERY WATERPROOF. HEAVY AND COLD WHEN WET.

HAND-KNITTED WOOLLY JUMPER

VEST

LONG JOHNS:
THEY'RE LIKE LONG BAGGY PANTS.

LONG OVERCOAT:
FOR THOSE REALLY NIPPY DAYS.

OXYGEN TANK:
VERY HEAVY AND BULKY.

ICE AXE:
AXE WITH A LONG WOODEN HANDLE MAKING IT DIFFICULT TO HANDLE.

MMM, DON'T THEY LOOK LOVELY!

HAND-KNITTED WOOLLY SOCKS

CANVAS RUCKSACK

HOB-NAILED BOOTS:
LEATHER BOOTS WITH STEEL NAILS IN THE SOLES FOR GRIPPING THE SNOW. HORRIBLY HEAVY AND UNCOMFORTABLE.

- reliable ropes: you might need to rope on to another person to cross a gruesome glacier. Or to go up a steep slope. So it's vital your rope's super-strong, and not about to break. Modern ropes are made of tough nylon. They're light, hardwearing and waterproof. (In the olden days, ropes were made from plant fibres. They froze when they got wet, making them hard to hold on to.) Some bits of Mount Everest have fixed ropes (they're always left in place). You clip or tie yourself on, then climb up.

- tent: you need a tent that's light to carry, strong and waterproof. Light metal tent poles are best. They'll bend a bit in high winds, so your tent doesn't blow away. Practise pitching your tent before you go. You won't have time to read the instructions on the mountain.

- sleeping bag

- food and drink: you'll need plenty to eat and drink. Climbing uses up loads of energy. Here's what you might eat on a typical day:

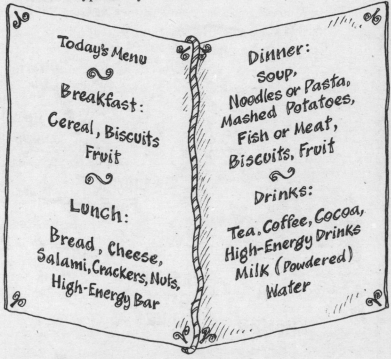

Today's Menu

Breakfast:
Cereal, Biscuits
Fruit

Lunch:
Bread, Cheese,
Salami, Crackers, Nuts,
High-Energy Bar

Dinner:
Soup,
Noodles or Pasta,
Mashed Potatoes,
Fish or Meat,
Biscuits, Fruit

Drinks:
Tea, Coffee, Cocoa,
High-Energy Drinks
Milk (Powdered)
Water

- a cooking stove, pots, cup, spoon and bowl

What you do:
1 Plan your route. The most popular route's up the South Face (that's the way Tenzing and Hillary went). You set up higher and higher camps until you reach the top. Hopefully. Each camp's stocked with spare supplies, equipment and climbers to back you up. It's a long, rocky road to get to the top. In case you get lost, here's a handy map to help you:

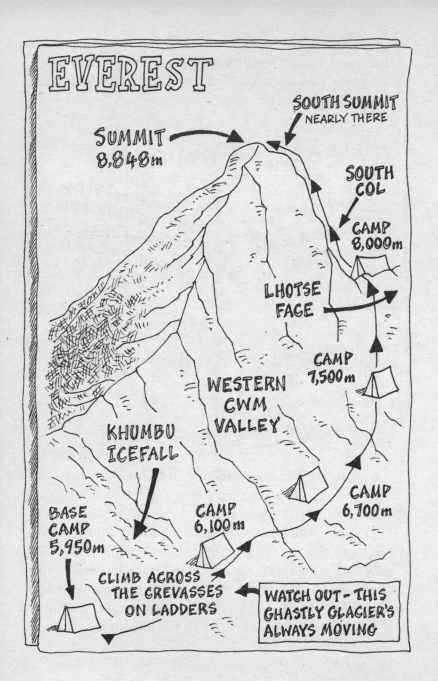

106

2 Ask permission. You'll need a permit to climb Mount Everest. At about £45,000, they're pretty pricey so start saving your pocket money now.

The best time to go is mid-May when the weather's good. Usually. Avoid the summer – you'll be swept away by the monsoon rains. The trouble is, peaky weather can change in a flash, catching you unawares. Always check the weather forecast before you set out.

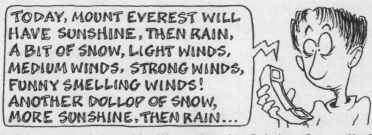

3 Get into training. You'll need to be fighting fit to climb Mount Everest. So if you're always trying to get out of games, you might want to give up now. A good way to get fit is to run up and down stairs, carrying a rucksack full of bricks. You'd better get used to it because you'll be lugging around loads of heavy gear. Running, swimming and weight training are also brilliant for building up your strength.

4 Choose your team. An expedition needs tonnes of gear just to keep it going – first you have to lug it to base camp, then higher and higher up. There's no way you can carry it all (even with all that weight training), so you'll have to hire some Sherpa porters and yaks to help you out. About 100 should do. Some Sherpas specialize in climbing high up – you can rely on them when the going gets really tough.

5 Get going. There's no time to lose. It will take you weeks to reach base camp. And even then, you're only half-way there. Don't forget to say your prayers before you set off to soften up the mountain gods. You're going to need all the help you can get… Good luck!

Teacher teaser

Tie your teacher up in knots with this harmless-sounding question. Put up your hand, smile, and say:

PLEASE, SIR THERE'S AN ALPINE BUTTERFLY IN SIMPKIN'S HAIR. SHALL I CATCH IT AND PUT IT OUT THE WINDOW?

Does your teacher tell you to get knotted?

Answer: Of course not. Teachers are much too polite. But you're nearer the truth than you think. An Alpine butterfly isn't an insect that flutters about or lands on people's hair, it's a type of knot. And it's horribly useful in climbing. You use it to tie yourself to a rope so you don't fall. Here's how you do it:

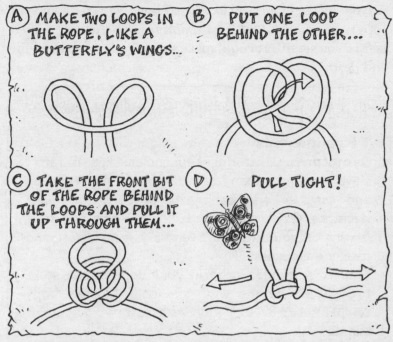

A) MAKE TWO LOOPS IN THE ROPE, LIKE A BUTTERFLY'S WINGS...

B) PUT ONE LOOP BEHIND THE OTHER...

C) TAKE THE FRONT BIT OF THE ROPE BEHIND THE LOOPS AND PULL IT UP THROUGH THEM...

D) PULL TIGHT!

Got all that? Good. You never know when you might need it.

HORRIBLE HEALTH WARNING

Mountains can be dangerous. More than 675 people have climbed Mount Everest ... and more than 160 never made it back down. If your teacher's serious about climbing mountains, make sure she goes to an expert for help. If she runs into trouble, she could call base camp on a solar-powered or satellite phone. Most expeditions carry them. Then if someone's badly injured, a rescue helicopter can be called in. But it can only land at base camp. Weather permitting...

Feeling peaky?

There are plenty of other horrible hazards waiting to freak you out on the mountainside. Don't leave home without your copy of the *Freaky Peak First Aid Manual*. Better still, read it before you set off. It could make the difference between life and death.

FREAKY PEAK FIRST AID MANUAL

1 Hypothermia

Symptoms: Chattering teeth and blue lips. You start shivering slowly, then faster and faster. You feel tired and sluggish, and can't talk properly, or make decisions. Oddly, you may feel very warm and start tearing off your clothes. Eventually you collapse and lose consciousness.

Cause: A sudden drop in your body temperature brought on by the wind and cold. Normal body temperature's 37°C. If it drops by just two degrees, it can be fatal.

Treatment: Wrap up warm and drink plenty of fluids to keep your circulation flowing. Eat plenty of sugary food for energy.

2 Dehydration

Symptoms: You feel thirsty, sleepy and sick. Then you get a headache. You can't walk or talk properly, and you don't know where you are. Can be fatal.

Cause: You lose loads of water as sweat as you climb. And the dry mountain air makes things worse.

Treatment: Drink plenty of water, even if you don't feel like it. If you wait until you feel thirsty, it may be too late. Whatever you do, don't eat the snow. It'll cool your body down even further. To tell if you're dehydrated, look at the colour of your pee. If it's light yellow, you're fine. If it's dark brown, you're in trouble.

WHAT HAPPENS WHEN IT'S PURPLE?

3 Snow blindness

Symptoms: Your eyes start to sting, then you see everything in shades of reddish pink. It's as if your eyes are full of gritty sand. Then you go blind for hours, or even days.

Cause: The glare of the sun's rays reflected from the ice or snow.

Treatment: Get into a dark place and cover your eyes with a damp, cooling cloth. Don't rub your eyes.

Better still, wear glacier goggles or strong sunglasses to protect your eyes from the glare, even when it's foggy.

STILL HAVING TROUBLE WITH YOUR EYES?

4 Frostbite

Symptoms: Attacks your fingers, feet, ears and nose. First they feel prickly, then numb. Later they turn red, swollen and blistery. Then they turn black and drop off.

Cause: Your skin and flesh get so cold, they freeze solid and die. Mild frostbite is called frostnip.

Treatment: Try to thaw out the frozen bits. Warning: this will be painful. Pull faces to stop frostbite freezing your nose. As a last resort, your fingers and toes may have to be amputated (cut off). Horrible.

5 Mountain sickness

Symptoms: Feels like a bad dose of flu, with headaches, sickness and loss of appetite. You feel tired but you can't go to sleep. You get a hacking cough and find it hard to breathe. You might even start seeing things.

Cause: Lack of oxygen high up. The trouble is, it can strike without warning once you're about 2,500 metres up. One minute you're feeling fine, the next you're hacking your guts up.

Treatment: Get down the mountain. Otherwise you could die. Or get into a Gamow bag (it's like a long, nylon tube you blow up with a pump). It'll release the pressure on your lungs. Then you can climb down.

Killer snows

Snow. You might think it's nice, white, fluffy stuff you see on Christmas cards. Think again. Believe it or not, snow can be a killer. Without any warning, thousands of tonnes of the stuff can roar down a mountain in an awful, awesome avalanche, sweeping away everything in its path – trees, people, cars, even whole villages. There's no escape from the dreaded white death, as this terrifying true story shows...

Galtur, Austria, 23 February 1999

Just before 4 p.m. on 23 February 1999, disaster hit Galtur in the Austrian Alps. The sleepy village, a popular skiing resort, was devastated by the worst avalanche to hit the region in 30 years. Villagers and visitors looked on helplessly as a massive wall of snow buried the village, bulldozering trees, houses and cars out of its way. Thirty-one people died; many more were badly injured. And half of Galtur was smashed into pieces. One survivor described the awful moment when the avalanche struck:

We had just gone into our hotel room when suddenly everything went black. There was no sound at all. Then something smacked against the window like a giant shockwave. Then you heard it hitting the other side of the hotel.

There had been no warning so people had only a few seconds to get out of the way. For some, there was no escape. Anyone buried under the snow stood only a very slim chance of survival. The only sign of the coming catastrophe was a thunderous roar as the vast slab of snow suddenly broke free and came crashing down the mountain. Besides, Galtur stood about 200 metres away from the base of the mountain so people thought it was safely out of reach of an avalanche. Small avalanches were a common sight but they usually trickled out long before they reached the village. Elsewhere in the valley, snow fences had been built across the slopes to slow the pace of any falling snow. But not around Galtur. No one thought they were needed there. No one expected the big one.

Scientists believed the tragedy was caused by freak winter weather in the Alps – some of the worst weather in living memory. In February alone, a record-breaking four metres of snow had fallen. Strong winds whipped the snow into dangerous drifts, pointing ominously towards Galtur. At any time, the snow could give way, with terrible consequences. It was a disaster waiting to happen. To make matters worse, roads and air links to Galtur had been closed for five days because of the atrocious weather. By the time the rescue teams finally arrived, some people had been buried in snow for 16 hours. Incredibly, 40 people were still pulled out alive. Against all the odds.

So what on Earth are avalanches? And how do these silent killers strike?

Some awful avalanche facts
1 An avalanche is a mass of mountain snow that suddenly breaks loose and crashes downhill. Galtur was hit by a "powder" avalanche. That's the type where tonnes of soft, powdery snow falls on to an icy layer. Then cracks begin to appear in the ice making the soft snow on top unstable – so unstable it suddenly starts to slip and slide.
2 For the snow to slide, it needs to be heavy enough to overcome friction (that's the freaky force that holds it to the rock). Then gravity does the rest. In Galtur, an astonishing 17,000 tonnes of snow hurtled down the mountainside. Which was bad enough. But by the time the avalanche hit

the village, it had picked up so much snow it had doubled in size. Imagine the size of that snowball!

3 Watch out if you're skiing. A number of things can trigger off a slide, including the weight of a single skier. Unfortunately, the peak avalanche season's January to March: the perfect time for skiing. The slamming of a car door can do the trick. Or even yodelling. Yes, yodelling. You know, that strange, high-pitched warbling sound? Well, in some Swiss mountain villages, yodelling is banned in spring when the avalanche risk is greatest. And village children aren't allowed to shout or sing either. Sounds a bit like a geography lesson.

4 Some avalanches move at high speeds of up to 320 kilometres an hour. Whoosh! That's as fast as a racing car. And they get faster the further they flow. The Galtur avalanche was going so fast, it took two whole minutes to come to a standstill. Doesn't sound much but that only gave people a measly 10 to 20 seconds to escape. Not long enough.

5 Believe it or not, in the First World War, avalanches were used as deadly weapons. Austrian and Italian troops fighting in the Alps aimed their fire at the mountain tops instead of at each other, triggering off loads of lethal avalanches. In 1916, 80,000 soldiers were killed in this way. In a single day!

6 Scientists are working hard to find a way to forecast when and where avalanches will strike next, so that a warning can be given. In the Alps, there are mini weather stations on each mountain top, measuring things like temperature, snowfall and rainfall. All crucial clues to avalanches. The scientists feed this data into computers and get them to come up with a forecast. So how good are they? The good news is they're getting better all the time. The bad news is it's not an exact science. You can't give a forecast for a particular valley, only for a whole region. And avalanches are horribly fickle.

7 So can anything stop an avalanche in its tracks? Well, various things have been tried. On some freaky peaks, steel fences are built across the slopes to hold the snow back. And houses are avalanche-proofed, with tough concrete walls and no doors or windows on the avalanche side. From time to time, experts deliberately use explosives to trigger off smallish slides. This helps avoid a dangerous build-up of snow. Sounds horribly risky, but it works. But the terrible truth is, once the snow gets flowing, there's no way on Earth you're going to get it to stop.

Cliff's top tips for avalanche safety

So if you're unlucky enough to be caught in an avalanche, what on Earth can you do? Unfortunately, your chances of survival are pretty slim. Around the world, avalanches kill about 200 people a year. Most suffocate to death as the snow sets solid around them, like icy concrete. Very nasty. But don't freak out. If a sinister snow slide's heading your way, try to remember these life-saving tips:

If you're caught in an avalanche...
- As the avalanche starts, try to get behind a shelter like a rock or a tree.
- Close your mouth so you don't swallow too much snow. And cover your nose with your hands. This will give you a bit of breathing space under the snow.
- Try to stay upright by waving your arms as if you're swimming. It might sound silly but it could save your life.

- When the snow stops, find out which way up you are by spitting. If the spit dribbles down your chin, you're upright. If it dribbles across your face, you're upside-down. If you can move, try to dig yourself out. In the opposite direction to the spit.

- Always carry a radio transceiver. It's a gadget you wear around your neck which will beep loudly so rescuers can find you under the snow.

If you're searching for someone...

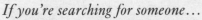

- Switch your transceiver to receive mode. Then you'll be able to pick up any signals for help.

- Search the area carefully for any clues. Use a long stick, called a snow probe, to prod the snow (gently) in case there's a body buried below.

- Take the dog for a walk. Dogs are brilliant at sniffing out victims because their noses are so sensitive. Forget posh high-tech equipment – dogs are by far the best.

- When you find someone, start digging them out straight away. There's no time to lose. Even after half an hour, most victims are dead. Uncover their mouth first so they can breathe. Then get them off the mountain, fast.

Freaky, isn't it? But DON'T PANIC. Remember, you're much more likely to be excused geography homework for the rest of your schooldays than be swept away by an avalanche. And how likely is that?

But never mind about climbing mountains because they are there. If horrible humans don't mend their ways, they might not be there much longer...

PEAK CONDITION

Despite all the dangers, it's official. Horrible humans are hooked on hills. But do freaky peaks like having them there? Or does all that tramping take its toll? Mountains might look as though they'll last for ever, but don't be fooled. They're far more fragile than they appear. Time to head off for Africa and freaky Mount Kilimanjaro…

Trouble on the mountain

Local Chagga people have lived on the slopes of Mount Kilimanjaro for hundreds of years. They believe the mountain's holy and treat it with great respect. After all, they say, you can't get closer to heaven than that. But it's more than just a mountain – its bubbling springs provide the Chagga with water for drinking and growing crops. Without it, they couldn't survive. But today the mountain's in grave danger. And with it the Chagga's traditional way of life.

In 1970, Kilimanjaro was turned into a national park to protect its stunning scenery. Thousands of tourists visit Tanzania each year for the thrill of climbing this freaky peak. It's a six-day hike to the top. The tourists bring in much-needed money and many of the Chagga get work as porters and guides. So far, so good. Trouble is, with around 18,000 hikers a year, not to mention 54,000 porters and guides, peaky Kilimanjaro is feeling the strain.

With so many climbers camping on the mountain, huge patches of forest have been cleared for firewood. And it only takes one careless spark from a camp fire to spark off a disastrous forest fire, leaving thousands of acres of mountain in ashes. It can take years and years for the trees to grow back again.

What's more, it's changing the lives of the Chagga too. They're being forced off their mountain, to live on the dry, dusty plains below. They used to hunt for food and graze their animals on the hillside. But they're not allowed to do this any more. Sadly, many are turning their backs on the mountain. Many people are very poor. So they cut down rare trees in the forest and sell the valuable wood for money. With fewer trees, the forests can't store water. Instead of seeping underground, any rain simply washes away. So there aren't as many mountain springs (you get these where underground water bubbles up to the surface), and the rivers are drying up. Which means people suffer even more because they don't have enough water for drinking and growing crops. It's a horribly vicious circle.

People are trying to put things right. They're planting more trees and limiting the number of trekkers. And children are learning to love the mountain as part of their geography lessons at school. Will it work? It's too early to say for sure. But it's worth it to save this breath-taking peak from going rapidly downhill.

Freaky peak fact file

NAME: Mount Kilimanjaro
LOCATION: Tanzania, Africa
HEIGHT: 5,895 metres
AGE: 500-300,000 years old
PEAK TYPE: Volcano (see page 27)
PEAKY POINTS:

• Kilimanjaro's the highest peak in Africa. It towers above the plains all around.

• Its name means "Shining Mountain" or "Mountain of Spring Water" in the local language.

• It's actually three freaky peaks joined together. There's Kibo, the highest, Mawenzi and Shira. Kibo's been dormant (sleeping) for the last 200 years.

• In 100 years' time, the great glaciers on Kibo could be gone for good. It's because the world's weather is getting warmer. They've already shrunk by half in the last century.

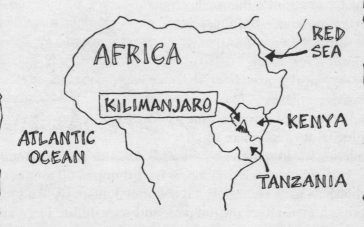

HORRIBLE HEALTH WARNING

It's not just Kilimanjaro that's under pressure. Things look bleak in the Himalayas too. Why? In Nepal so many trees have been chopped down for firewood, many slopes have been stripped bare. And without any tree roots to cement the soil together, it's easily washed away. Apart from the danger of serious landslides, the soil's causing problems by silting up the mountain rivers. This causes fatal flooding further downstream.

High-rise rubbish

Mountaineers have a saying: when you climb a mountain, any mountain, don't leave anything but footprints behind. Sensible advice. Freaky peaks are horribly sensitive places. The last thing they need is you making a mess. But guess where you'll  find the world's highest junkyard? On the top of Mount Everest, where careless climbers have dumped 60 tonnes of rubbish. That's enough to fill about 600 dustbins. And it's having a fatal effect on the peak and its wildlife. Here are some of the freakiest things you might find…

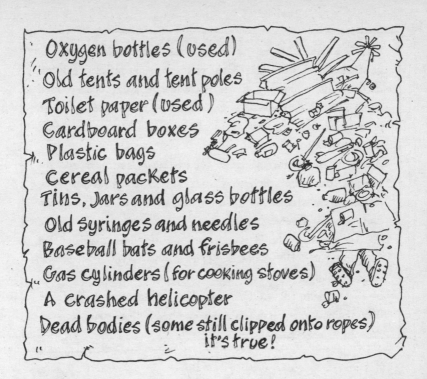

Oxygen bottles (used)
Old tents and tent poles
Toilet paper (used)
Cardboard boxes
Plastic bags
Cereal packets
Tins, jars and glass bottles
Old syringes and needles
Baseball bats and frisbees
Gas cylinders (for cooking stoves)
A crashed helicopter
Dead bodies (some still clipped onto ropes)
it's true!

Peak protection

Mountains are certainly in a bit of a mess but things aren't all gloom and doom. Campaigns are underway to spring clean the mountains. Why not start up one of your own? If you find yourself up a freaky peak, do your bit to keep it in peak condition. Don't know where to start? Over the page are a few simple rules to follow:

1 If you're making a fire, use as little wood as possible. And put the fire out properly afterwards.

2 Burn or bury any litter that'll rot away (like paper and, yes, dead bodies). Pack the rest up and take it home. Today, if you drop litter on Mount Everest, you're in for a hefty fine.

3 Keep mountain streams sparkling clean. After all, they're used for drinking water. So don't wash your dishes in a stream or use it as a toilet. Dirty water can spread deadly diseases.

4 Don't pick the flowers or dig up the plants. And don't disturb the animals. Things are tough enough for peaky wildlife without you making it worse.

5 And finally ... 2002 was the International Year of Mountains. Why not go and give a hill a hug. Go on, nobody's looking...

A peaky future?

So what does the future hold for freaky peaks? Nobody really knows. But one thing's for certain: mountains will carry on growing and shrinking. Little by little, every year. And there's nothing anyone can do about it. As the Earth's pushy plates continue to move, it'll be goodbye to many of the peaks we know. Sounds freaky. But it won't happen overnight. As you know, mountain building takes millions and millions of years. (Quite soon in geographical time but not soon enough to get you out of your field trip.) At the same time, brand-new mountains are always being born. And, experts reckon, these freaky peaks could grow even higher than sky-scraping Mount Everest. Now *that's* amazing.

OOOH, LOOK! THERE'S THAT TITCHY MOUNT EVEREST, WAY DOWN THERE

If you're interested in finding out more about freaky peaks, here are some websites you can visit.

www.thebmc.co.uk
The British Mountaineering Council's website.

www.mnteverest.net
Statistics, quotes and information about planning expeditions to Mount Everest.

www.everestnews.com/
More news from the top of the world, with weather reports and information about expeditions in progress.

library.advanced.org/10131
This site focuses on the Himalayas and is full of freaky facts about their history, geology and the dangers facing them from climbers and pollution.

www.americasroof.com/
This site covers every high mountain right across the USA and gives loads of details about how to hike up one.

PERISHING POLES

INTRODUCTION

Geography lessons. Snow laughing matter, are they? Some geography teachers freeze you to the spot with their brain-numbing knowledge of all kinds of weird words...

TODAY'S LESSON IS ABOUT GLACIATION*. LET'S START WITH GELIFLUCTION* AND MOVE ON TO POLYNAS*.

ICY STARE

BRRR...!

*Roughly translated, glaciation is the tricky technical term for how a place gets covered in ice. Gelifluction's the way frozen ground moves and sinks when the ice melts out of the soil in spring. Polynas are patches of water surrounded by sea ice. I bet you wish you'd never asked!

JELLY WHO?

POLLY WHO?

But chill out! It could be worse. Much worse. If you thought your classroom was horribly damp and chilly, thank your lucky stars you don't go to school at the f-f-freezing North or South Pole. You'd be so bloomin' busy keeping warm, you wouldn't have time to moan.

The bad news is that the parky Poles are the coldest, iciest and driest places on our whole perishing planet. They're also some of the windiest. And they're horribly far away. In fact, they're at the ends of the Earth and you can't get much further than that. Jolly good riddance, you might say. But you'd be wrong. The good news is that the perishing Poles are one of the most brilliant bits of geography ever. You'll soon be bitten by the polar bug (if the frostbite doesn't get you first).

Getting cold feet? Don't panic. The great thing about *Horrible Geography* is that you can visit far-flung places without having to leave home. This book is ideal for armchair travellers. Just like you. So find a comfy armchair, chill out and get stuck in. Just think how impressed your teacher will be with your new-found polar know-how. And you don't even need to pack an ice-pick.

If you're itching to know what it's really like at the Poles (without having to get up), try this simple experiment. Wait for a really cold winter's day. I'm talking the sort of day when you need a snow plough just to get out of your front door. The sort of day when going to school is COMPLETELY OUT OF THE QUESTION! Then send your little sister outside. (Call her in again after a few minutes. DON'T FORGET.) Look at your sister closely. Is she **a)** covered in goose pimples, **b)** frozen solid, or **c)** the proud owner of a blue nose?

If the answer is all of them, you'll have some idea of what it's like at the poles. (Don't worry – your sister won't be able to snitch. Her teeth will be chattering too much.)

And that's what this book is all about. Yes, colder than the coldest deepfreeze, and covered in ice several kilometres thick, the Poles are the coolest places on the planet. In *Perishing Poles*, you can...

• learn how to drive an Inuit dog sledge.

• search for deep-frozen mammoths buried under the ice.

- make a delicious dip from the contents of a caribou's stomach.
- track an iceberg the size of Belgium with ice-cool glaciologist*, Gloria.

N-ICE TO MEET YOU.

* A glay-see-olo-gist is the posh name for a scientist who studies ice. Thank goodness someone knows what your teacher's wittering on about.

This is geography like never before. And it's horribly exciting. But be warned – wrap up warm before you start reading this book, even if you're staying indoors. You're about to embark on an icy adventure that'll send shivers down your spine.

RACE FOR THE POLE

1 November 1911, McMurdo Sound, Antarctica

In the perishing morning cold, the small team of men shook hands with their companions and said their goodbyes. Their mood was solemn. Would they ever see their friends again? No one knew. For they were about to embark on the biggest adventure of their lives. They were trying to become the first people to reach the South Pole, and earn a place in history. A horribly hazardous journey lay ahead of them across the icy Antarctic wastes. One man had seen it all before. Nine years earlier, expedition leader, Captain Robert Falcon Scott, had come within a few hundred kilometres of the Pole, before freezing cold weather and howling winds forced him back. This time steely Scott was determined to succeed, or die in the trying.

Preparations for the journey lasted almost a year. But on 1 June 1910, Scott's ship, *Terra Nova*, an old whaling ship which had been refitted and strengthened to break through the ice, finally left England. Six months later, after a stormy passage, *Terra Nova* moored in McMurdo Sound, among the drifting pack ice. Scott and his men built a hut on the beach at Cape Evans on Ross Island and settled in for the long, dark days of winter. (In the Southern Hemisphere, the seasons are the other way round. So from March to October, it's winter at the South Pole.)

Braving the treacherous temperatures, they busied themselves laying supplies on their route to the Pole and conducting scientific experiments. In the evenings, they listened to gramophone records and watched slide shows to help pass the time. So far, so good.

Now, at last, the waiting was over. The time had come to strike for the Pole. As he said his goodbyes, sombre Captain Scott looked cool and calm, but his thoughts were racing. He had left London safe in the knowledge that his greatest rival, the brilliant Norwegian explorer, Roald Amundsen, was at the other end of the Earth, heading for the Arctic. Amundsen was hoping to reach the North Pole first, leaving the South Pole to Scott. Or so he thought. On 6 April 1909, American Robert Peary claimed to have reached the North Pole, scuppering Amundsen's plans. Without telling anyone, ambitious Amundsen immediately changed course and headed south instead of north. The first thing Scott knew about it was a telegram from Amundsen which read:

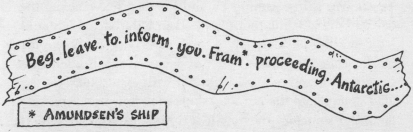

Beg. leave. to. inform. you. Fram*. proceeding. Antarctic...

* AMUNDSEN'S SHIP

But by that time, Amundsen was already on his way. There was no turning back for either of them. The race for the South Pole was well and truly on. Ten days after Scott's arrival, Amundsen and his party landed at the Bay of Whales, on the Ross Ice Shelf, and set up their camp (called Framheim). Everything had gone according to plan. While Scott and his men were saying goodbye, Amundsen was already well under way.

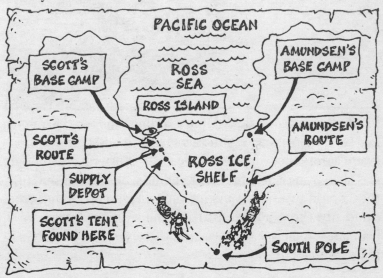

December 1911/January 1912

By the time Scott left Cape Evans, Amundsen was 12 days in front of him. And his lead was lengthening. By 17 November, gritty Amundsen and his men had reached the halfway mark at the foot of the Transantarctic Mountains. Now another obstacle lay in their path – a steeply sloping glacier, called the Axel Heiberg Glacier. It was riddled with treacherous crevasses, and littered with giant blocks of ice. The struggle up the perilous slope took four back-breaking days. But somehow they made it to the top. Now all that lay between them and the Pole was a vast expanse of dazzling white ice (called the polar plateau), stretching as far as the eye could see.

Then disaster struck. Almost at once the weather broke. For two terrible weeks, blinding blizzards and howling winds swept across the plateau. All the gutsy Norwegians could do was shelter in their flimsy tent behind a block of ice and pray they would be saved. Luckily, their prayers were answered. Suddenly, the wind dropped and the weather cleared. With brilliant sunshine and blue skies, the rest of the journey was plain sailing.

On 14 December, Amundsen and his hardy companions stood at last at the South Pole. Without a word, the men shook hands. There was no need to say anything. They'd made it – that was enough. But they did not dare stay very long. As they knew to their cost, the weather could change at any time. Amundsen spent three days fixing his position accurately, using a sextant (that's an old-fashioned instrument for navigating by measuring the angle between the horizon and the sun) to prove to everybody he had really made it. Before leaving, the men pitched a tent and planted a Norwegian flag on top. Amundsen also left a note for Scott, asking him to forward news of their triumph to the king of Norway. The note read:

> Dear Captain Scott,
>
> As you probably are the first to reach this area after us, I will ask you kindly to forward this letter to King Haakon VII. If you can use any of the articles left in the tent, please do not hesitate to do so. With kind regards.
> I wish you a safe return.
> Yours truly, Roald Amundsen

Six weeks later, the Norwegians returned to Framheim, fighting fit and well. They had completed their epic 2,500-kilometre journey in a staggering 98 days.

Meanwhile, Scott was in desperate trouble. As Amundsen proudly posed for photos at the South Pole, Scott and his men were struggling up another treacherous glacier, called the Beardmore Glacier, almost 640 kilometres away. Finally, on New Year's Day 1912, they too reached the polar plateau. Now, at last, the end was in sight and their spirits rose. Little did they know that Amundsen was already on his way home. For his final strike on the Pole, Scott picked four trusty companions – Edgar Evans, Lawrence Oates, Henry Bowers and Dr Edward Wilson. The rest of the support team was sent back. It was a superhuman effort. With temperatures plunging below an icy –40°C, every step was agony.

But worse was to come. On 16 January, the men spotted a black flag in the distance. And it seemed to be marking a camp. Amundsen had beaten them to it. Their worst fears had come true. In his diary, Scott summed up their dashed dreams:

"The worst has happened, or nearly the worst... The Norwegians have forestalled us and are the first to the Pole. It is a terrible disappointment... Tomorrow we must march on to the Pole and then hasten home with all the speed we can compass."

Bitterly disappointed, Scott reached the Pole two days later. "Great God!" he wrote in his diary. "This is an awful place."

The return journey

Exhausted, starving, suffering from frostbite and with their spirits broken, Scott and his men began their nightmare journey home. Drifting snow covered their tracks and they frequently lost their way. One by one, the men's strength began to fail. On 17 February, Edgar Evans died after a fall into a crevasse. A month later, brave Lawrence Oates walked out of the tent into a blizzard. "I am just going outside," he said. "And may be some time." It was the last time they saw Oates alive. His feet were so badly frostbitten that he preferred to die alone rather than slow his companions down.

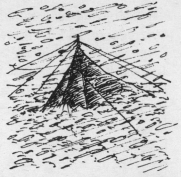

On 19 March, with food and fuel rations running dangerously low, the three survivors, Scott, Wilson and Bowers, found themselves trapped in their tent by a blinding blizzard. Howling gales and whirling snow made it impossible to battle on. Just 18 kilometres away lay a supply depot stocked with food and fuel that would have saved their lives. But it remained tantalizingly out of reach. For days, the men waited for the weather to clear but they knew in their hearts they were doomed. Each day, they grew weaker. With the last of his strength, Scott wrote letters home and kept up his diary. The last entry was dated Thursday, 29 March 1912. He wrote:

Thursday, 29 March, 1912

Since the 21 March we have had a continuous gale. We have had fuel to make two cups of tea a piece and bare food for two days. Every day we have been ready to start for our depot, but outside the door of the tent it remains a scene of whirling drift. I do not think we can hope for any better things now.

We shall stick it out to the end, but we are getting weaker, of course, and the end cannot be far.

It seems a pity, but I do not think I can write more.

R. Scott

The following November, a search party found the snow-covered tent, and the three bodies inside it. Scott's diary and letters lay beside him. A snow cairn with a cross made from skis was built over the spot.

Five frostbitten reasons why Amundsen reached the South Pole first

1 He had a head start. Amundsen pitched camp right at the edge of the Ross Ice Shelf – a pretty risky thing to do. If the ice had broken off, his camp would have drifted out to sea. But it was a risk worth taking. It meant Amundsen was already about 100 kilometres closer to the South Pole than Scott. By the time Scott finally set off, Amundsen was a long way ahead.

2 He let husky dogs do all the hard work. They were fast, well trained and tough. Six top-notch dogs could pull a half-tonne sledge up to 100 kilometres a day. At first, the men rode on the sledges, then were pulled along on skis. Scott had little experience of using dogs. He also thought it was manlier for his men to pull the sledges themselves, even though it was back-breaking work. One man wrote that it felt like his insides were being jerked out. The going was too tough for the ponies Scott brought all the way from Siberia. The poor beasts sank up to their knees in the snow and their sweat froze on their fur. To put them out of their misery, the ponies were eventually shot. As for the expedition's three motorized sledges – two broke down and one was dropped overboard as it was being unloaded.

3 His men ate fresh meat. Amundsen knew that without supplies of fresh meat his men would die of scurvy (that's a deadly disease caused by a lack of vital vitamin C). So when supplies ran out, he did the dirty on the dogs. At a place called "The Butcher's Shop", on the polar plateau, he had half the dogs (over 30) shot dead. Some of them ended up as dog-meat, while the men had fresh dog cutlets for dinner. Squeamish Scott thought eating dogs was horribly cruel. His staple diet was pemmican (a ghastly mixture of dried beef and lard) and oatmeal porridge with the odd penguin or seal steak thrown in. Trouble was, pulling sledges used up loads of energy and there wasn't enough to eat. While Amundsen's team was well fed from the start, Scott's men ran out of vitamins and slowly starved to death.

4 He studied the Inuit people. Amundsen had learned crucial lessons from the local Arctic people about surviving the teeth-chattering cold. He had his clothes made from wolfskin, following an Inuit design. They kept the men warm and dry, even when temperatures plunged below -40°C. Scott, on the other hand, preferred clothes made from cotton and wool. The snag was they weren't warm enough and didn't allow sweat to escape. So the men ended up freezing cold *and* sopping wet.

5 He wasn't bothered about science. Amundsen's aim was simply to reach the South Pole. So he hand-picked a team of top polar experts for the gruelling journey. They included expert dog handlers and sledge drivers, and a super-fit ski champion. Amundsen himself began to train as a doctor but gave it up to explore instead. (As a kid in Norway, he'd dreamed of reaching the South Pole. He even slept with his windows open in winter to toughen himself up for the trip.) Scott, meanwhile, was dead keen on science. He loaded his sledges with heavy rock samples which made

144

them horribly hard to pull. (Actually, the rocks turned out to be crucial clues and showed Antarctica used to be much warmer than it is today. Sadly, this startling discovery came too late for poor Scott.)

6 He had all the luck. On his return journey Scott was faced with freak cold weather. Instead of the usual temperatures of -30°C, Scott had to cope with temperatures which plunged below -40°C. Meanwhile, Amundsen was safely back at base.

It's a fact, then. The Poles are perilous places to be. As plucky Captain Scott found out to his peril, you need to be horribly tough to survive in the bitter cold. Think *you* could take them on and still come out alive? First you'll need to get to know the Poles better. A lot better...

THE PARKY POLES

Imagine miles and miles of ice and snow, as far as the eye can see. Add some battering blasts of wind, and some freezing cold temperatures. It's like peeking inside the biggest, coldest deep freezer on Earth – but without the frozen chips and ice lollies. Welcome to the parky Poles.

Pole position

Forget maypoles, flag-poles and tent poles, these aren't that sort of pole. No, they're actually the very ends of the Earth, at either end of the Earth's axis (that's an imaginary line running down its middle). This means you can only go south from the North Pole, and from the South Pole everywhere is north. Confused? Don't be. Here's Gloria with handy polar diagram no. 1.

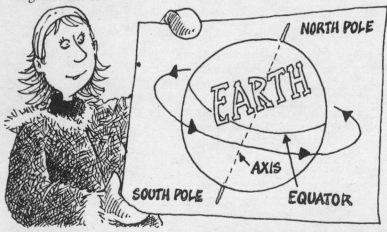

To muddle matters more, horrible geographers call the regions that surround the North Pole the Arctic, and the regions that surround the South Pole the Antarctic or Antarctica. Together they cover a chilly eight per cent of the Earth's surface.

Time for handy polar diagram no. 2.

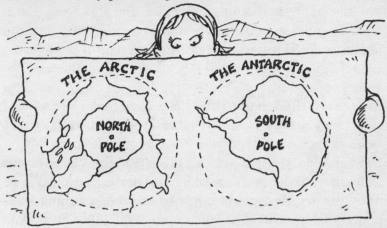

But you can't blame horrible geographers. Oddly enough, it was the ancient Greeks who first thought up the names. Bet you didn't know that "Arctic" comes from the Greek word for, er, bear? Only this polar bear wasn't white and furry. And it didn't hunt seals on the ice. No, this was a bear-shaped pattern of stars that shone over the North Pole. And "Antarctic" simply means opposite the bear.

Actually, the globe-trotting Greeks never went near the Antarctic so how on Earth did they know it was there? The terrible truth is, they didn't. It was all down to guesswork, and the Greeks were brilliant at that. They reckoned there must be a lump of land at the bottom of the world to balance out the lump at the top. Otherwise, the top-heavy Earth would topple over. Incredibly, they were right – but not about the Earth toppling over. Antarctica really does exist.

Poles apart

You might think both parky Poles look much the same. I mean they're both freezing cold and icy, right? But actually, beneath their icy exterior, the Poles are worlds apart. So how on Earth do you tell which Pole is which? Getting your Poles in a puzzle? Not sure which end of the Earth you're at? Why not try this ice-cold quiz to tell the perishing Poles apart. All you have to do is answer NORTH POLE, SOUTH POLE or BOTH to each question. Ready?

1 It's a continent covered with ice.
2 It's a piece of frozen ocean.
3 There are polar bears but no penguins.
4 In summer, the sun shines all night.
5 In June, it's the middle of winter.
6 People live here all year round.

Answers:
1 SOUTH POLE. Underneath all that ice, there's a colossal continent lurking. Antarctica covers 14 million square kilometres – that's almost twice the size of Europe. But 99 per cent of it is capped by a gigantic sheet of ice, nearly 5 KILOMETRES THICK in places. That's enough to reach halfway up mighty Mount Everest. The ice is so bloomin' heavy, the land's sunk beneath its weight. And that's not all. Buried beneath the awesome ice are massive mountains and violent volcanoes. Luckily,

most of them are extinct – but one freaky peak, Mount Erebus, could blow its top at any time.

Antarctica's completely surrounded by the Southern Ocean. In winter, around a third of the ocean freezes over, increasing Antarctica's size. **Warning**: don't fall overboard when you're on your next polar expedition. This stormy sea's so perishing cold your brain would freeze solid in a matter of minutes. Brrrr!

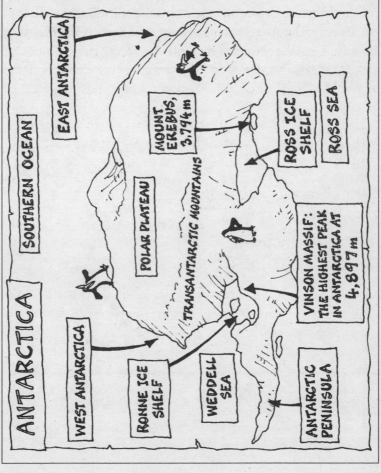

2 NORTH POLE. There isn't any land at the North Pole, only frozen ocean. The Arctic Ocean's the world's smallest ocean (it covers 14,000,000 square kilometres), and the chilliest (watch out, brain!). For most of the year, it's covered in drifting ice up to 3 metres thick. The Arctic Ocean's almost entirely surrounded by land. This includes the northern parts of Canada, Alaska, Scandinavia and Russia, together with glacial Greenland. Together they make up the region geographers call the Arctic. So the Antarctic's land surrounded by sea, and the Arctic's sea surrounded by land. Got all that?

ARCTIC

CANADA

RUSSIA

NORTH POLE
•

GREENLAND

ARCTIC OCEAN

EUROPE

3 NORTH POLE. There are no penguins at the North Pole. You might bump into a polar bear but if a penguin pootles past you, you're at the wrong perishing Pole!

ARE YOU SURE I'M LOST?

TRUST ME!

4 BOTH. If you can't get to sleep... (so no change there, then). The Sun doesn't rise for weeks on end and it's dark all the time. At the South Pole in winter, it's dark for six months on end. Why on Earth does this happen? Well, as the Earth orbits (circles round) the sun, it spins once on its axis, every 24 hours. The Earth's axis also tilts over at an angle. This means that some places on Earth tilt towards the sun and others tilt away, so some places have longer hours of daylight. This is why the length of the days and nights changes throughout the year.

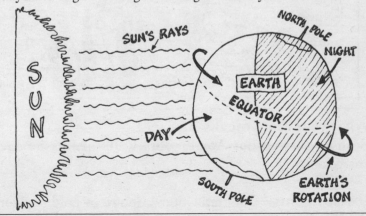

SUN'S RAYS

SUN

EARTH

EQUATOR

DAY

NORTH POLE

NIGHT

SOUTH POLE

EARTH'S ROTATION

5 SOUTH POLE. While you're lazing about on the beach during your summer holidays, it's winter at the South Pole. And when it's winter in the north, it's summer down south. If you see what I mean. This is because, in June, the northern hemisphere tilts towards the sun and has summer. But the southern hemisphere tilts away from the sun and has winter. And in December, you get the reverse.

6 BOTH. Local people have lived in the Arctic for years and years. And they're experts at surviving. (You can meet some of them in **Perishing Polar People**.) But it's a different story at the South Pole. Only a few horribly hardy scientists live there all year round. It's just too bloomin' cold. And they're a very long way from home. Your nearest neighbours live in South America, about 3,000 kilometres away. Never mind, you'll have millions of penguins to keep you company.

What your score means...

So how did you do? Award yourself 100 points for each correct answer.

500-600 points. Congratulations! You're in pole position. But don't get carried away. Next thing you'll be suggesting a perilous polar field trip to your teacher. Perish the thought.

300-400 points. Not bad. You're obviously warming to your subject. But be careful – you could still slip up on the ice.

200 points and below. Terrible. You're really skating on thin ice. You'll never be a geographical genius at this rate. But if you really can't tell your Poles apart, here's a simple diagram to help. You'll need to turn the book upside-down to spot the South Pole, or stand on your head…

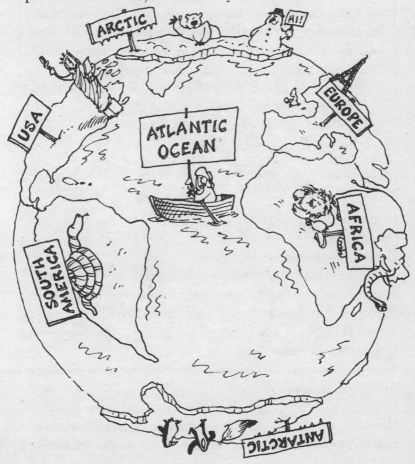

Polar weather report

Planning a personal polar expedition? Best check out Gloria's perishing polar weather forecast before you venture out…

Today will start off bitterly cold with temperatures well below freezing. Expect gale-force winds in the afternoon with the likelihood of a blizzard. And watch your step in winter, it will be pitch black all day. Tomorrow will be much the same, and the next day, and the day after. Summer might be a bit warmer (if you can last out that long, and at least you'll be able to see where you're going).

Polar weather warning

If you thought it was chilly in winter where you live, think again. The perishing Poles are absolutely f-f-f-freezing. Whatever time of year you pick, you'll need to wrap up warm. IF YOU WANT TO STAY ALIVE. The forecast for the forseeable future is:

Teeth-chatteringly cold

It's official. The perishing Poles are the coldest places on Earth. At the South Pole, the average temperature is a teeth-chattering -49°C, that's about five times colder than inside your freezer. But quite toasty compared to a place called Vostok where temperatures plummet as low as -89°C. Now that's plenty cold enough to freeze you to death. It's a lot warmer at the nippy North Pole, a toasty 0°C in mid summer (though it's -30°C in winter). But why on Earth are the Poles so bone-chillingly cold? Sorry, horrible science lesson alert... It's because the Earth's surface curves and so the sun's rays hit the Poles at a wide angle. They spread out over a wide area, which makes them weaker. The sun's rays also have to take a longer path through the Earth's atmosphere to reach the Poles. So some heat's soaked up or scattered by the atmosphere before it even hits the ground.

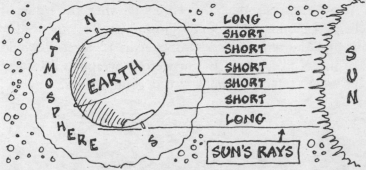

What's more, most of the sunlight that strikes the Poles is reflected straight back by the white ice. Horrible geographers call this the albedo effect. Put simply, it means that dark colours soak up heat while white reflects heat away. And it's why wearing a white T-shirt on a hot day keeps you cooler than wearing a black one. Try it for yourself and see.

Wild and windy

Watch out for wind at the perishing Poles. Seal steaks can play havoc with your insides. (Only joking. It's not that sort of wind.) This sort of wind can howl down the icy slopes at a staggering 200 kilometres per hour, as fast as a train. Fast enough to knock you off your feet. Or batter you with a blinding blizzard. A blizzard's a savage snow storm whipped up by the wind. Woe betide you if you're caught up in one. It'll blast snow into your mouth so you can't breathe, and make it impossible to see. And it's one of the main reasons polar explorers get hopelessly lost, often with tragic results. Worse still, the wind makes it feel far chillier than it actually is. You see, the stronger the wind's blowing, the colder it feels. And get this. If the wind's blowing at 50 kilometres per hour and the temperature's -35°C, the wind chill would make it feel like -80°C. If you weren't wrapped up warm you'd freeze solid in seconds. Pretty grim, really...

Dry as a bone

Strictly speaking, geographers count the South Pole as a desert. No, their brains haven't turned into icicles. This isn't the sort of desert you're thinking of, with sizzling sand dunes, palm trees and camels. But it's a desert all the same. Geographers describe a desert as a place which gets less than 250 millimetres of rain or snow each year. And Antarctica gets only a fifth of that. Even though it's covered in frozen water,

parts of Antarctica are even drier than the bone-dry Sahara Desert. In some places, such as the dry valleys near McMurdo Sound, no rain has fallen for two million years.

Earth-shattering fact
The perishing South Pole was once warm and tropical. Believe it or not. Scientists found fossils of the same plants and animals in ancient rocks from Australia, South America and Antarctica. They showed that 200 million years ago these continents were joined together. Amazingly, Antarctica was covered in lush, green forests where dinosaurs roamed about. Then, about 180 million years ago, the three continents split apart and became separated by sea. South America and Australia stayed toasty warm. But Antarctica drifted to the South Pole and got colder and icier.

Awesome aurorae

If you're out and about during the long winter nights at the North Pole, and you suddenly see bright, flashing lights in the sky – DON'T PANIC. It isn't an alien spaceship on a mission to abduct your teacher (you wish). No, this spectacular polar light show is called the aurora borealis*. It happens when electrical particles stream from the sun and bash into gases in the Earth's atmosphere. Oh, so you knew that already? Well, in the past people hadn't a clue what caused the awesome aurorae. So they made up stories to make sense of what was going on.

> *Roughly translated, aurora borealis means "northern lights". Aurora's the old Roman name for the goddess of dawn and borealis means northern. At the South Pole, you get southern lights, or aurora australis.

WICKED!

1 The Inuit people of Canada thought the sky was a dome stretched over the Earth. Holes in the dome let light in and the spirits of dead people out. They believed the aurorae were blazing torches that guided the spirits to heaven.

2 The Vikings believed the northern lights were the breath of heavenly warriors. When they died, they fought out battles for ever in the sky.

3 Other people found the lights frightening. They thought (wrongly) that they spread death, disease and war. It was best not to mess with them in case they turned nasty. This meant not waving, whistling or staring. Else they might reach down and grab you. Bet you're scared.

A mammoth discovery

Warning: while you're busy ogling the aurora, watch your step. You might be about to stumble on a truly gigantic, and I mean mammoth, surprise. You might not know this but hundreds of prehistoric woolly mammoths (like enormous hairy elephants) have been found deep-frozen in the rock-hard Siberian ground. (It's so bone-chillingly cold the ground never thaws out so it's known as permafrost.) They've been buried for thousands of years since before the last Ice Age. Some are so well preserved you can still see their shaggy, red hair, and even cook and eat them. At a banquet in Russia in the 19th century, defrosted mammoth steak was the dish of the day. Fancy a mouldy mouthful?

There's just one tiny problem – before you can tuck into your monster dinner, you'll have to defrost it first. Here's how to do it.

A mammoth task

What you need:

- A deep-frozen mammoth, about 20,000 years old
- Some tools – shovels, pickaxes, drills and jackhammers
- A helicopter
- Lots of hair-driers
- A large oven and deepfreeze
- A gas mask

What you do:

1 First, find your mammoth. But wrap up warm – snowbound Siberia's the best place to look for this beast.

2 Dig up the mammoth. This might be easier said than done. The frozen ground's as hard as concrete, but your jackhammer should do the job.

3 Lift the mammoth out of the ground. You'll need the helicopter for this bit. Make sure it's tied on tight – this unusual ice cube weighs a mammoth 20 tonnes.

4 Choose a nice, cold place to keep your mammoth, like a massive deepfreeze or an ice cave. That way, it won't melt and go mouldy as you chip the ice away.

5 Defrost the mammoth with the hair-driers. But be warned. This is a horribly tedious task and could take you months or years. (Never mind. Think of all those ghastly geography lessons you're going to have to miss. And you'll need your gas mask as your mammoth defrosts. It'll make a terrible pong.)

6 For a roast dinner with a difference, cook your mammoth in a giant oven (cooking time: one week). Then serve it up with some veg and gravy, and add tusks to decorate. Simple!

Before you rush off to recover from your mammoth tusk, sorry, task, here's a quick question. What's cold, white and slippery? No, it isn't disgusting school dinner rice pudding. Give up? Well, without it, glaciologists like Gloria would have to look for another job. What is it? Ice, of course.

THE TIP OF THE ICEBERG

Some people think ice is boring. I mean, apart from deep-freezing mammoths and cooling down drinks, what on Earth is frozen water good for? It's about as much use as a chocolate teapot. But not as tasty. But there's much more to ice than meets the ice, sorry, eyes, as you're about to find out.

Could you be a glaciologist?

Some horrible geographers like Gloria spend their whole lives studying ice. What d'ya mean, you'd rather watch a mammoth defrost? Could you be a cool glaciologist? If you think one lump of ice looks just like another, you'd better dip into Gloria's *Which Ice?* guide and get to grips with the different ice types.

Which Ice?

Ice sheet
Description: A vast sheet of ice that covers Antarctica and Greenland.
How it forms: From snowflakes which fall on the ground and get squashed by more snow falling on top. Slowly, air gets squeezed out of the snow and it turns into ice. But it takes thousands and thousands of years.

Got some spare time on your hands? Why not make your own ice sheet? All you have to do is make a few ice cubes – about 1,000 MILLION MILLION MILLION should do. That's how much ice is frozen in the awesome Antarctic ice sheet. Oh, by the way, you'll need a deepfreeze twice the size of Australia to keep your ice sheet in.

Glacier
Description: A gigantic river of ice.
How it forms: From ice that flows from the centre of an ice sheet. To look at, an ice sheet seems horribly solid. But oddly, the ice is like runny icing on a birthday cake. It flows out from the middle of the sheet and moves slowly towards the sea. The record-breaking Lambert Glacier in Antarctica is a staggering 515 kilometres long and over 40 kilometres wide. That's one big birthday cake. Luckily, this gigantic glacier creeps along at a snail's pace, at about 2.5 centimetres a day.

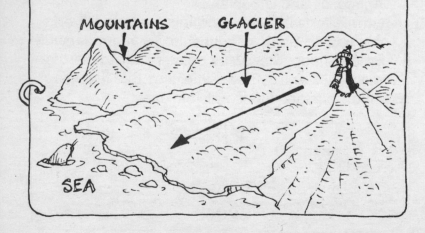

MOUNTAINS   GLACIER

SEA

Ice shelf

Description: A massive slab of ice that is attached to the land but which floats on the sea.

How it forms: From an ice sheet or glacier that flows out to sea. The shelf stays fixed to the ice sheet and icebergs break off the end and float away. Ice shelves can be enormous. The Ross Ice Shelf in Antarctica is about the same size as the whole of France.

Sea ice

Description: A Thin layer of ice over the sea.

How it forms: From frozen seawater. The Arctic Ocean and some of the Southern Ocean freezes solid in winter. In fact, winter sea ice almost doubles the size of Antarctica. It's only a few metres thick and mostly melts away in summer. Pack ice consists of broken bits of sea ice that drift on the wind and ocean currents. The sort of sea ice that clings to the coast is called fast ice. All horribly hazardous to ships.

But these four cool customers are just the tip of the iceberg. You'll have to visit Gloria's Uncle Gino's polar ice-cream parlour to check out the rest. Go on, you deserve a treat. Choose from six sensationally frosty flavours. They're guaranteed to melt in your mouth.

Uncle Gino's ICE CREAM
You'd go to the ends of the Earth for it!

① FABULOUS FRAZIL ICE
A slushy mixture of needle-shaped ice crystals which float in the water.
Great for slurping through your teeth.

② PERFECT PANCAKE ICE
Round and flat like pancakes, only much crunchier. These pancakes float on the sea. Grab one as the sea starts to freeze over for winter. For wide-mouthed customers only.

③ GOURMET GREASE ICE
A soupy mush of sea ice which gives the surface of water an oily sheen. For slippery customers.

④ SUNCUP SPECIAL
A gigantic ice sculpture carved from snow by the waves and wind. Looks like an enormous mushroom. Our vegetarian offering.

⑤ SASTRUGI WHIP
Ice that's been whipped into peaks and troughs by the wind. A bit like the yummy topping on a lemon meringue pie.
Hold on to your hats!

⑥ ICEBERG EXTRAVAGANZA
Today's special, this is an ice lolly like you've never had before. One of these beauties will keep you quiet for years and years. WARNING: SEE FACT SHEET BEFORE YOU START LICKING!

167

Eight freezing iceberg facts

1 Icebergs are colossal chunks of ice that break away from glaciers and ice shelves. And we're not talking one or two here but thousands every year. Oddly, horrible geographers call this breaking off "calving". So you'd think a baby iceberg would be called a calf wouldn't you. But, for some reason, it isn't. Glaciologists call baby icebergs growlers. But don't worry, their bark's usually worse than their bite (the glaciologists', I mean).

2 Growlers are about the size of grand pianos which is titchy in iceberg terms. The next bergs up are called bergy bits (yes, really!). They are the size of houses, but even that's pretty paltry. Some awesome icebergs are real monsters. In Antarctica, they're like enormous ice islands and can measure a staggering 150 kilometres long and 150 metres tall. This is how awe-struck Arctic explorer, Admiral Richard E. Byrd, described his first sight of icebergs:

Stricken fleets of ice bigger by far than all the navies in the world, wandering hopelessly through a smoking gloom.

3 Incredible icebergs come in all sorts of shapes and sizes. Here's a quick spotter's guide to the main sorts. Can you spot the odd one out?

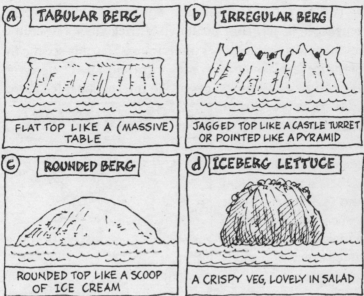

(a) TABULAR BERG
FLAT TOP LIKE A (MASSIVE) TABLE

(b) IRREGULAR BERG
JAGGED TOP LIKE A CASTLE TURRET OR POINTED LIKE A PYRAMID

(c) ROUNDED BERG
ROUNDED TOP LIKE A SCOOP OF ICE CREAM

(d) ICEBERG LETTUCE
A CRISPY VEG, LOVELY IN SALAD

4 The biggest iceberg ever was spotted off the coast of Antarctica by the crew of the USS *Glacier*. In 1956, they had the fright of their lives when a monster berg THE SIZE OF BELGIUM went floating by. Imagine an ice lolly that big! Luckily, they lived to tell the tale.

5 Which is more than can be said for the passengers and crew of the supposedly unsinkable RMS *Titanic*, the most luxurious ocean liner ever built. In April 1912, the *Titanic* was on her maiden voyage from Southampton to New York, sailing across the North Atlantic with more than 2,000 people on board. It was late at night and the sea was icy. By the time the lookouts spotted the iceberg dead ahead, it was too late to get out of the way. The lethal berg gashed a huge hole in the ship's side and water began pouring in. A few hours later, the *Titanic* sank with the tragic loss of 1,490 lives.

6 Trouble is, icebergs are horribly tricky to spot because seven-tenths of the ice lies underwater. You only see the tip of the iceberg. So they can easily rip a ship apart before you even know it. Today, planes of the International Ice Patrol scan the icy Arctic seas, warning ships of iceberg danger. And scientists also track icebergs with radar and satellites. Some icebergs are even fitted with radio transmitters to tell scientists exactly where they are.

I'M BEHIND YOU!

7 Keeping tabs on an iceberg sounds simple enough. But icebergs don't hang around for very long. Big bergs can drift for thousands of kilometres on the wind and ocean currents. And they're always giving scientists the slip. Icebergs from the Arctic have been seen as far south as balmy Bermuda. Most icebergs last for about two years before they break up and melt. But some can stay frozen solid for up to 20 years…

I'M MELTING IN THIS HEAT!

8 Which could be horribly useful for humans. If you melted a medium-sized berg, you'd have enough water to supply a big city for weeks. Great news for dry places like Australia and the Middle East which get very little rain. There's just one teeny snag. How on Earth do you lug the iceberg all that way in one piece? Scientists think huge supertugs could be built to tow the icebergs from Antarctica. This would take about a year. Are the scientists serious? Would their crackpot scheme really work? It's probably much too costly to put into practice, but you'll have to wait and see. For the time being, their plans are on ice.

Earth-shattering fact
In Japan and Arctic Canada, companies are now selling chunks of glacier ice for cooling down trendy drinks. When the ice melts, it gives off bubbles of air which have been trapped in the ice for thousands of years. How cool is that?

Teacher teaser
Next time your teacher asks you an awkward question, ask him this one back. Smile as if a glacier ice cube wouldn't melt in your mouth, and put up your hand and say:

He'll be so gobsmacked, he'll forget what he asked you. But what on Earth are you talking about?

Answer: Incredibly, the answer is yes, it can! To find out more about ice, glaciologists drill deep holes and pull out long sticks of ice, like giant ice lollies, which they call ice cores. By counting the layers in the ice, they can tell how old the ice

OOOH! HALF PAST SIX!

is. Scientists recently drilled an ice core 3 kilometres long in Antarctica. They reckon the ancient ice at the bottom is a staggering 250,000 years old. Core blimey!

HELP! IT'S A NUNATAK!

No, no, no. It's nothing to do with nuns. A nunatak is (noon-attack) a polar peak or island that pokes out above the ice sheet. Actually, it comes from a local Inuit word for attached land.

For intrepid British explorer, Sir Ernest Shackleton (1874–1922), nunataks were the least of his worries. If he never saw ice again in his life, it wouldn't be a day too soon. Now that your teeth have stopped chattering, check out this amazing true tale…

Icebound in Antarctica, 1914–1917

SHACKLETON

As a lad, Sir Ernest Shackleton dreamed of seeing the world. You could say adventure was in his blood. He was only 16 when he left school and ran away to sea. Later, he went to nautical college and became a master sailor. He almost reached the South Pole twice (once with Captain Scott) but had been beaten back by woeful weather. Now he wanted to be the first person to cross the icy Antarctic continent. But first he needed a crew. The story goes that he put an advert in the paper:

> Men wanted for hazardous journey,
> Small wages, bitter cold.
> Long months of complete darkness,
> Constant danger, safe return doubtful.
> Honour and recognition in case of success.

Would you have signed up? No way? Luckily for Ernest, applications flooded in. And from 5,000 hopeful volunteers, he picked the pluckiest. On 1 August 1914, he and his crew of 28 men set sail from England on board their sturdy ship, the *Endurance*. Ahead of them lay a desperate journey across the most hostile habitat on Earth. A journey no one had ever tried before. Their last port of call before Antarctica was the tiny island of South Georgia. Then it was south into the unknown.

In December, the *Endurance* sailed into the treacherous, ice-infested waters of the Weddell Sea. Battling through the perilous pack ice was no picnic. For weeks, they tried to find a clear channel through the constantly drifting ice floes. But their efforts were in vain. Then, on 19 January 1915, disaster struck. The *Endurance* stuck fast in the pack ice, just one day's sail from their destination at Vahsel Bay. Soon she was frozen solid, "like an almond in a piece of toffee", one man wrote.

As the pack ice dragged *Endurance* ever further away from land, Shackleton knew his dream was over. Summer was nearly gone – it would be impossible to cross the continent now, even if they could reach it. They would have to spend winter on the ice.

At first, the ship was safe enough for the men to live on board. But for how long? Nobody knew. One of two things might happen. Come spring, the ice might thaw and free the ship. Or the shifting ice floes could crush it to pieces, like a fragile eggshell. (An ice floe's a chunk of floating sea ice.) By October, the signs were ominous. With a rumbling sound like thunder, the floes tightened their icy grip. Before the crew's disbelieving eyes, the *Endurance* began to break up.

Her timbers groaned and cracked under the pressure, and she sprung leak after leak. As she listed to one side, Shackleton gave orders to abandon ship. The men salvaged what they could, including the three lifeboats, and pitched camp on the ice. Their only hope was that the ice would carry them within reach of land. Otherwise, the future looked horribly bleak. With no radio contact, no one knew where on Earth they where.

Some weeks later, on 21 November, Shackleton and his men watched sadly as the *Endurance* sank beneath the ice.

Nightmare at sea

For months, the men drifted on the ice. But by April, it was obvious the ice was splitting up, right beneath their feet. At any minute it could give way – their camp was no longer safe. Shackleton ordered the lifeboats to be launched – they would try to make for land, however desperate the journey was. And desperate it was. They braved icebergs and gale-force winds that could tear a boat to pieces. The men took it in turns at rowing. But by the end of the watch, their hands were so icy cold they had to be chipped from the oars. At night, they camped on the ice floe, until it became too dangerous. One night, a gigantic crack suddenly opened up and a man plunged into the perishing sea in his sleeping-bag. Shackleton managed to haul him out but they'd learned their lesson. After that they slept in the lifeboats. At last, after an appalling six-day journey, they reached a rocky island called Elephant Island on the Northern Antarctic Peninsula and stumbled on to the stony, ice-covered beach. It was the first time the men had set foot on solid land for 497 days.

But their celebrations didn't last long. On this isolated island, there was no hope of rescue. No one ever came near this awful place. What's more, another wretched winter was looming... Shackleton knew there was only one thing for it. He would have to go for help. Taking five men with him, Shackleton set out in one of the lifeboats. It was a horribly risky thing to do. He decided to head back to South Georgia and its whaling station, some 1,200 kilometres away ... across the stormiest seas in the world. For days, the men fought to keep their little boat afloat as it was tossed by giant waves and tearing winds. It was so cold the sea spray froze on the boat, caking it in thick ice. Despite the constant pitching and rolling, the men had to risk their lives chipping it off. Otherwise the boat would have sunk.

The only shelter from the weather was a canvas cover stretched over the bow. But conditions inside were hellish.

There was only enough space for three men to go in at a time. And it was wet, cramped and bitterly cold. Like being buried alive.

Frostbitten, exhausted and sodden, and with just two days' water left, it seemed they couldn't last long. Then, after 17 desperate days at sea, a piece of seaweed floated by – a sure sign of land!

But they weren't safe yet. With South Georgia in their sights, the weather suddenly changed for the worse. Hurricane-force winds drove them towards the sheer cliffs, threatening to smash the boat to pieces. It took a superhuman effort, but somehow they managed to steer into a cove.

The last leg
There was just one small snag – the whaling station lay on the far side of the island. And it was too risky to sail round. There was only one answer: some of them would have to set out on foot. It was a terrible setback for the exhausted men who were already on their last legs. As the crow flies, the whaling station was only 35 kilometres away. But it might as well have been on the moon. No one had ever attempted to cross the island before – and there were no useful maps. Between them and the station lay perilous peaks, capped

with glaciers and pitted with killer crevasses. But it was a risk they had to take. On 19 May, Shackleton set out with two men, a rope, an ice-axe and three days' supplies stuffed into their socks. For extra grip, they banged nails from the boat into the soles of their boots. Then, for 36 exhausting

hours, the three men slogged on, hardly daring to stop and rest. One false step and they'd plummet into the icy sea and certain death.

At last, on the afternoon of 20 May, they stumbled into the whaling station. Against all the odds, they'd made it. Filthy and wild-looking, Shackleton approached the startled manager.

"My name is Shackleton," he said.

It turned out they'd reached safety just in time. That night, a biting blizzard blew up that would have killed them if they'd been caught in it. Later that year, Shackleton sailed for Elephant Island to rescue his stranded men. Incredibly, despite their appalling ordeal, not a single life had been lost.

Test your teacher
Ernest Shackleton would have made a brilliant teacher. He was intelligent, brave, cheerful and a born leader. What a hero! What d'ya mean, that doesn't sound like any teacher you know? He was also one of the most famous explorers ever. So famous that even your own geography teacher will know all about him. In fact, it's probably his specialist subject. Try this quick quiz to find out.

1 Shackleton's ship was called *Endurance*. Why?

a) It was an old family motto.

b) It came from the back of a cereal packet.

c) It was the name of a famous sea battle.

2 On the way to Antarctica, the ship's cat, Mrs Chippy, fell overboard. What did Shackleton do?

a) Left it to perish.

b) Turned round and went back for it.

c) Threw it some ship's mice to eat.

3 What was Shackleton's nickname?

a) Bossy Boots.

b) Grumpy Drawers.

c) The Boss.

4 What did Shackleton's parents want him to be?

a) A doctor.

b) An explorer.

c) A vet.

5 Which of these books did Shackleton write?

a) *Perishing Poles.*

b) *South.*

c) *The Heart of the Antarctic.*

HMM, PESKY POLES?
PARKY POLES?
PURPLE POLES?
TENT POLE?

One thing's for certain. Getting to grips with awesome ice is a risky thing to do. If your ship isn't smashed to smithereens, you might end up in the freezing drink. Count yourself lucky. You can always nip off home and have a nice, hot drink while you thaw out your frostbitten feet. The hardy creatures you're about to meet are well and truly left out in the cold.

LIFE IN THE FREEZER

Some people think they're real tough nuts. You know the sort I mean. In winter, while you're wrapped up like an Egyptian mummy, they're wearing a vest and telling everyone how brilliantly hot it is.

But are they really as hardy as they seem? What if the temperature was a f-f-freezing -20°C? And what if it was accompanied by pitch darkness, and spine-chilling winds? Perfect polar conditions, in fact. Surely nothing could live at the ends of the Earth without freezing to death?

Incredibly, for hundreds of horribly hardy plants and animals, the perishing Poles are home, sweet home. How on Earth do they survive in their hostile habitat? Why not drop in at the world's first (and only) perishing polar pet shop…

HORRIBLE HEALTH WARNING

Some of these pets can be horribly dangerous. Especially if they're hungry. So if you're thinking of training them to fetch your slippers or use the remote-control, DON'T BOTHER! By the way, your new polar pet will need a nice, cold place to live, preferably outdoors. If you keep it in the house, turn off the central heating. If it gets too hot, it'll die.

Perishing polar pet shop

Are you a lonely geographer? Are you looking for a little friend, someone to snuggle up to on those nippy polar nights?

Look no further! For your perfect pet, visit our Polar Pet Shop. We guarantee you won't find any fluffy bunnies or gormless goldfish here…

The Ice fish has got antifreeze in its blood, like the stuff your dad puts in the car in winter. This stops the freaky fish from freezing to death. Now is that cool, or what?

And don't worry if you forget to feed your fish. It's used to going hungry. In the icy ocean, food's sometimes hard to find. No wonder this unfussy fish will guzzle anything, given half a chance.

① ENT-ICE-ING ICE FISH:
DESCRIPTION: A SEE-THROUGH FISH WITH GREAT BIG TEETH, A BIG SNOUT AND BIG EYES. A BIT LIKE A FISHY GHOST.
SIZE: YOU'LL NEED A WHOPPING TANK FOR THIS PET - IT CAN GROW 60 CENTIMETRES LONG.
HABITAT: SOUTHERN OCEAN.

The Arctic fox is perfectly colour co-ordinated. In summer, it grows a thin, brown-grey coat to match the tundra* rocks. It's the perfect disguise for sneaking up on its prey. In winter, it changes into a thick, white coat to blend in with the ice and keep it warm. In summer, small furry creatures called lemmings are this cunning creature's favourite snack. In winter, the fox follows polar bears and scoffs their left-overs.

POLAR CHUNKS
POLA CHU
POL CHU

PENGUIN PELLETS
PENGUIN PELLETS
PENGUIN PELLETS

②FABULOUS ARCTIC FOX.
DESCRIPTION: ER, LIKE A FOX ACTUALLY. (WELL WHAT DID YOU EXPECT?) HABITAT: ARCTIC SEA ICE AND TUNDRA.

* The tundra's a vast stretch of icy wasteland around the North Pole. It's covered in short, scrubby plants but it's too cold for trees to grow. In winter, the top of the tundra's frozen but it thaws out in summer.

Despite their lousy appearance, isopods make fascinating pets. For a start, they grow, and move, very slowly (thank goodness for that!). That's because the water's so icy cold, they need to save energy and there's not much food about. It feeds on seabed scraps, including worms, sea-bed creatures and lumps of nourishing seal poo.

③ ENORMOUS ISOPOD:
DESCRIPTION: LIKE A GIANT, AND WE MEAN **GIANT** WOODLOUSE.
SIZE: 17 CENTIMETRES LONG (AS LONG AS TEN ORDINARY WOODLICE).
HABITAT: SOUTHERN OCEAN SEABED.

I'D HATE TO FIND ONE OF **THEM** IN MY PYJAMAS!

You might have trouble keeping track of the globe-trotting Arctic tern - it loves travelling. It escapes the northern winter blues by spending summer in Antarctica. Then it heads back to the Arctic for summer again. That way, good weather is guaranteed and it picks up a fish supper or two on the way. Fancy packing your bags and tagging along? It's a round trip of 40,000 kilometres.

④ GLOBE-TROTTING ARCTIC TERN:
DESCRIPTION: WHITE BIRD WITH A BLACK HEAD, BRIGHT RED BEAK AND LONG FORKED TAIL. SMALL, BUT CUTS A DASH. HABITAT: ARCTIC AND ANTARCTICA.

⑤ SLINKY WEDDELL SEAL: DESCRIPTION: LARGE AND LUMBERING WITH A SMALL HEAD AND BIG EYES. SLEEK GREY COAT WITH BLACK AND GREY SPOTS. SIZE: 3 METRES LONG AND WEIGHS UP TO HALF A TONNE. HABITAT: THE SEA ICE AROUND ANTARCTICA.

The Weddell seal mostly lives under the ice where it's warmer. It uses its teeth to gnaw breathing holes in the ice. (No wonder they're always falling out.) A thick layer of blubber (fat) under its skin keeps it warm. It feeds on deep-sea fish and squid. Luckily, seals are brilliant deep-sea divers and can hold their breath for an hour while they're hunting for food. (DON'T try this at home, however peckish you feel.)

The Polar Pet Shop presents
☆ CREATURE OF THE WEEK ☆

THE POLAR PET SHOP IS PROUD TO PRESENT THIS WEEK'S CREATURE OF THE WEEK...THE COOLEST POLAR PET AROUND...THE PERISHING

☆ POLAR BEAR ☆

DESCRIPTION: HUGE WHITE BEAR!

SHARP TEETH: FOR GRABBING AND CHEWING PREY (WATCH OUT YOU'RE NOT ON THE MENU)

SMALL HEAD AND EARS: FOR CUTTING DOWN HEAT LOSS

LONG NOSE: FOR HEATING THE FREEZING AIR BEFORE IT REACHES THE BEAR'S LUNGS AND FOR SNIFFING OUT SEALS

WHITE FUR: FOR CAMOUFLAGE ON THE ICE

FURRY PAWS: LIKE SNOW-SHOES FOR WALKING OVER SOFT SNOW WITHOUT SINKING THEY'RE ALSO PADDLE-SHAPED FOR SWIMMING

SHARP CLAWS: FOR KEEPING A GRIP ON THE SLIPPERY ICE AND SWIPING AT SEALS

THICK FUR COAT: FOR KEEPING OUT THE COLD. THE HAIRS ARE HOLLOW FOR TRAPPING THE SUN'S HEAT, AND OILY TO KEEP THE BEAR WATERPROOF. UNDERNEATH, THERE'S A THICK LAYER OF BLUBBER (FAT) FOR WARMTH. HANDILY, THIS CAN ALSO BE CONVERTED INTO FOOD AND WATER

If you're thinking of getting a polar bear as a pet, here's a word of warning. Looking after a polar bear isn't easy. Forget saucers of milk or little fishy treats. Polar bears are no pussy-cats. Still keen? OK, here are some handy hints and tips on polar-bear care.

POLAR BEAR PET-OWNER'S MANUAL

• Get a really BIG bed for your new pet. In fact, get a really big house – polar bears are massive. I've come across bears on my travels that weigh a tonne and stand a towering three metres tall (that's about twice as tall as you). Imagine taking that for a walk! They're the biggest, most powerful carnivores (meat-eaters) around so my advice to you is: keep clear of those seriously sharp teeth.

• Take your bear to the swimming pool. Your polar bear will need plenty of exercise. But forget walkies. Polar bears are superb swimmers (they do a sort of doggy paddle). And they can keep it up for days. Don't worry if your bear goes missing. When they fancy a rest, they hop on an ice floe and drift off, sometimes for hundreds of kilometres.

KEEP UP!

• Stock up on seal steaks. Ordinary pet food won't do. Polar bears love juicy seal steaks or better still, juicy whole seals. Polar bears are sneaky hunters. They wait by a seal's breathing hole, covering their black noses with their paws for extra camouflage. Then, when a seal pops up for air, the bear bashes it on the head. Nice! A sharp-nosed bear can sniff a seal out over a kilometre away, even if it's lurking beneath the ice.

SNIFF!
SNIFF!

• House-train your polar bear. If you dare. They've got some horrible habits, I can tell you. When there isn't much food about, they come into town and rummage about in people's dustbins. In Churchill, Canada, pilfering polar bears are such pests, they're rounded up and put in a polar bear jail! Frequent offenders are given a sedative to make them sleepy and carried away by helicopter. They're taken off somewhere safe, a long way from the town.

• Don't be fooled by their cute appearance. Polar bear cubs look sweet, don't they? Especially on Christmas cards. But looks can be deceptive. They might be all wide-eyed and fluffy now but, like puppies and kittens, they soon grow up. And they start learning to hunt almost as soon as they can walk. So if you're going to try cuddling a polar bear cub, expect a nasty nip or two. Ouch!

Earth-shattering fact

There aren't any polar bears in Antarctica. In fact, there aren't any big land animals at all. It's too parky for them to live. The largest year-round resident is a minute flightless midge. This titchy insect's just 12 millimetres long – that's this big:

In case you were wondering, there's no point in the midge having wings because it's too bloomin' windy to fly. Even teenier mites (they're close relations of spiders) live up seals' nostrils. Great if they could be trained to pick their noses too.

P-p-p-pick up a penguin

If you don't have room for a polar bear, and mites are a mite irritating, why not p-p-p-pick up a penguin instead. Now you might think a penguin's a silly-looking bird that looks as if it's dressed up like a waiter in a posh restaurant. And of course, you'd be right. But when it comes to staying alive in the bitter cold, plucky penguins are no bird brains. Take the emperor penguin, for example.

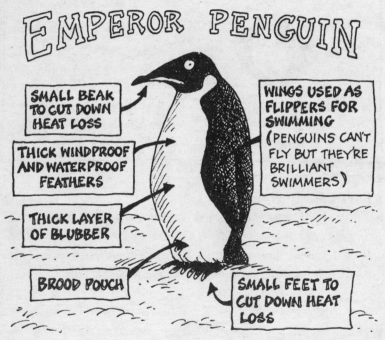

EMPEROR PENGUIN

SMALL BEAK TO CUT DOWN HEAT LOSS

WINGS USED AS FLIPPERS FOR SWIMMING (PENGUINS CAN'T FLY BUT THEY'RE BRILLIANT SWIMMERS)

THICK WINDPROOF AND WATERPROOF FEATHERS

THICK LAYER OF BLUBBER

BROOD POUCH

SMALL FEET TO CUT DOWN HEAT LOSS

A cold snap doesn't rattle an emperor penguin. They're much too tough for that. In fact, they find the freezing temperatures so bracing they spend the winter on the Antarctic ice when the weather's at its worst. Their babies are even born there. Imagine you were an emperor penguin chick. Would you be able to survive?

Could you be an emperor penguin?

1 You start off life as a large egg about 12 centimetres long which your mum lays on to her feet. Then she scarpers. She heads off to sea to hunt for fish while your dad's left holding the baby.

2 Your dad balances the egg on top of his feet and covers it with a furry flap of skin. The flap's called a brood pouch, and it keeps the egg warm and snug. If it falls on to the freezing ice, the chick inside will die.

3 And there your dad stays for 60 days and 60 nights without food or shelter. Even though the temperature may drop to -40°C and he's battered by blizzards. Brave, isn't he? But your dad's not the only one. He joins thousands of other males who huddle together for warmth.

4 You hatch out in the middle of winter. Brrr! Your dad carries you about on his feet until you're about eight weeks old. Then you grow a thick, fluffy feather coat to keep you warm.

5 Your doting dad hasn't eaten for months and he's horribly skinny and thin. Luckily, your mum comes back. Just in the nick of time. Your ravenous dad waddles off to sea for a well-earned feast, while your mum sicks up some fish for your supper. Lovely.

6 By mid-summer, you're old enough to look after yourself. You leave home and head out to sea for some fishing. But watch out for leopard seals lurking at the edge of the ice. Their favourite meal is, guess what? Yep, young penguins.

Life in the polar seas

You need to be seriously tough to survive on land, but it's a different story in the polar seas. Even though the water's bitterly cold, it's teeming with life. That's because there's plenty of food for peckish polar creatures to guzzle. The animals in the sea are joined in a food chain. That's the name horrible scientists use to describe the links between animals and the creatures they gobble. Most food chains start off with plants. A typical food chain goes something like this:

A food chain in the perishing Southern Ocean goes something like this:

① ALGAE — TINY SINGLE-CELLED PLANT

② KRILL — TINY SHRIMPS THAT GRAZE ON ALGAE

③ BLUE WHALE — THE BIGGEST ANIMAL EVER (EAT YOUR HEART OUT DINOSAURS) LOVES TO GUZZLE KRILL

The secret diary of a krill

Krill are little pink shrimp–like creatures a paltry five centimetres long. Real small fry. So you might think it would take an awesome amount of krill to fill a blue whale up. And you'd be right. Blue whales have truly enormous appetites. They can eat a staggering FOUR TONNES of krill … EVERY DAY. Imagine eating that much school dinner! And they're not the only ones. Greedy sea birds, penguins, seals and fish also gorge themselves silly on krill. So you see krill are vitally important in the polar food chain. But what's it like for the krill? I mean, it can't be much fun being chased around all day, then gobbled up for lunch. What if a krill could keep a secret diary? (OK, so you're really going to have to stretch your imagination for this bit…)

my secret diary by A.Krill

The Southern Ocean, Midsummer

1 p.m. Spent lunchtime swimming around with mates, minding own business. Felt a bit peckish so stopped off for a scrumptious snack of ice algae.

1.10 p.m. Huh! Just about to grab a snack when a blue whale blundered by. Bloomin' big mouth. Why can't they pick on someone their own size? And talk about terrible table manners. They swim along with mouths wide open (don't they know it's rude?).

1.20 p.m. Got swept up in its great gob, the big bully. Made lucky escape with some of me mates, but unlucky ones got strained out of the water. Whale lunch. What a way to go. No fun being a krill, I can tell you. You need eyes in the back of your head.

Later that day...

3 p.m. Aaaagghh! Here we go again. It's coming to get me. And its big, fat mouth is watering. I want my mummy!

A few minutes later...

Note: Sadly, that was the last entry in the krill's diary. This time, its luck ran out. Did the blue whale care? Did it, heck! After all, there were plenty more fish in the sea.

Krill swim about in massive swarms, weighing up to ten million tonnes each. These swarms are so huge they can be spotted by ships' radar and even by satellites in outer space. Scientists reckon there are about 600 million million krill in the Southern Ocean (that's 100 times as many people on Earth). Which makes them pretty tough for blue whales to miss.

HORRIBLE HEALTH WARNING
Fancy tucking into a nice plate of sausage and chips? Krill sausage and chips, that is. And what about krill and cream cheese sandwiches? Believe it or not, krill cuisine is catching on fast with horrible humans. Trouble is, you'd need to scoff it down fast – krill goes off very quickly. Phwoar!

Plucky polar plants

Most plants love warm, sunny weather with the odd light shower of rain. They're perfect conditions for plants to bloom. Conditions you'd never get at the perishing poles. You might think that faced with the cold, dry and windy conditions polar plants would curl up and die. But surprisingly, some plants manage to grow in them. Here's the low-down for all those plants out there who might be thinking of emigrating:

1 Don't bother with soil. Some Antarctic algae (tiny single-celled plants) have got little hairs for swimming in the snow. That way they can reach the sunlight which they need for making food. And to stop their bodies freezing, they make a kind of antifreeze. In some places, algae turn the snow bright pink, like raspberry ripple ice cream. The plants' red colouring works a bit like suncream and stops them getting sunburnt in the super-strong polar sun. Ingenious, eh?

2 Don't be fussy about what you eat. Lichen are ideal plants for the poles because they'll even feed on bare rock. The lichens make acids which dissolve the rock and make it crumble. Then they send out tiny "roots" to suck up nourishing goodness from the rock. They use this to make food. Other lichens live on seal or penguin poo left on the rock. Lovely!

3 Learn to live anywhere. Some Antarctic algae actually live inside solid rock. These picky plants prefer dark-coloured rocks which soak up the sun's heat (it's the albedo effect again). They're also out of the biting wind. The algae creep into the rock through minute cracks. They're kept alive by sunlight filtering through the see-through grains in the rock.

4 Grow as slowly as possible. That's how lichens survive the bitter cold. At the perishing poles, there may only be one day every year when it's warm enough to grow. So a patch of lichen the size of a cabbage leaf may be hundreds of years old. Even soggy school dinner cabbage isn't that old!

5 Forget flowering in winter. It's too bloomin' dark and cold. But when spring comes, polar flowers burst into bloom. Mind you, they have to be quick and spread their seeds before the next cold snap bites.

6 Keep your head down. Polar trees aren't tall and bushy like the trees you see outside. In fact, they're so small you could step right over the top. Trees, like Arctic willows, grow very low and spindly to keep out of the howling wind. Like long-lived lichens, they grow in slow motion. A willow stem as thick as a pencil may be hundreds of years old. (By the way, there aren't any trees in Antarctica at all.)

But bird-brained penguins, whopping whales and pint-sized polar trees aren't the only weird wildlife you'll find at the poles. Some humans find the freezing conditions rather refreshing, in fact. Are they stark, raving mad or just very well wrapped up? Why not nip along into the next chapter and meet up with a few of them?

GOING MY WAY?

PERISHING POLAR PEOPLE

Polar living may be cool for polar bears. But what about human beings? Astonishingly, some hardy humans actually choose to live near the North Pole, despite the horribly hostile conditions. So how on Earth do these polar people cope with their icy lifestyle? Who better to ask than the local Inuit people of the Arctic. They've lived on the ice all their lives.

By the way, no one lives permanently at the parky South Pole – it's just too teeth-chatteringly cold. But you might bump into the odd batty Antarctic scientist or two a bit later on in this chapter.

A TAXI

Polar people

The Inuit (Ee-noo-eet) mainly live in icy Alaska, northern Canada and Greenland. In the Inuit language, their name means "the people". Traditionally, the Inuit roamed the Arctic, fishing and hunting animals for food. Their lives were ruled by the changing seasons. In summer, they hunted seals, whales and walruses near the coast, and stocked up with food for winter. In winter, they moved inland to hunt caribou (reindeer). The Inuit relied on the land and sea for everything they used, and treated their icy home with great respect, taking care not to do any harm.

So how on Earth do the Inuit do it? Are you ready to find out how they survive? If you're planning on paying the Inuit a visit, be warned. You might think you've got it tough with too much homework and too little pocket money. But at least you don't risk freezing to death every time you nip out of your front door. Living in the Arctic is horribly hard. The Inuit know the ice like the back of their hands, and they're experts at polar survival. Even so, one false move and they, and you, could easily be a goner.

If you want to learn to live like a local, why not sneak a look in our essential Inuit Polar survival guide. It's packed full of life-saving hints and tips. Just ask good old Gloria – she wouldn't leave home without it.

Teacher teaser

Is your teacher always showing off about how many languages she can speak? Boring, isn't it? Try this tongue-twisting teaser to get your own back. When your teacher asks for your homework, smile sweetly and say:

PLEASE, MISS. I HAVEN'T FINISHED IT. YOU SEE, MY QARASAASIAQ'S ON THE BLINK

Do you need to see the doctor?

Answer: No, there's nothing wrong with you. Qarasaasiaq's the word for computer in the Inuktitut language (that's the lingo spoken by the Inuit). It's made up of three words which mean "little artificial brain". If the Inuit don't have word for something, they simply make one up. Do you take sugar in your tea? Then you'll need to ask for some siorasat "looks like sand". Clever, eh?

Perishing Polar Survival for Beginners by the Inuit

Lesson 1. What to wear

If you're heading off to the perishing Poles, you need to dress for the part. But forget looking cool. It's keeping warm that counts. And chucking on an extra jumper won't do, I'm afraid. (Even if your dear old granny knitted it for Christmas.) You need to wear layers of clothes that'll trap warm air next to your skin, and let sweat escape (otherwise it'll draw the warmth away and could freeze on your skin). To stay really warm and snug, take a look at what the locals are wearing. Then model your clothes on theirs. Here's the best in Inuit cool.

This is a traditional Inuit costume which was worn for hundreds of years. Today, many of the Inuit buy modern clothes from a company called the Hudson's Bay Company or by mail-order instead.

NICE!

Earth-shattering fact
An anorak isn't a really naff mac worn by nerds, whatever you might think. In the Inuit language, an annuraaq's *the word for a really cool coat – well, a really warm one actually.*

CARIBOU SKIN COAT:
Worn fur side out. Animal skin is brilliantly warm and windproof. Wear a thinner sealskin or bird skin tunic underneath with the furry side turned towards your skin.

FOX OR WOLF FUR TRIM AROUND HOOD:
Stops your breath freezing on your skin.

POLAR BEAR SKIN TROUSERS:
Worn fur side out. Tuck into your boots to keep out draughts. Wear a thinner pair of sealskin or fox fur trousers underneath, fur side in.

SEALSKIN MITTENS: You can also pull your hands inside your sleeves to stop your fingers getting frostbite.

MUKLUKS: (Sealskin boots) With a pair of sheepskin or sealskin socks worn underneath, fur side facing in. If it's very cold, wear several pairs of boots, one on top of the other.

Bootiful boots

If you fancy a new pair of trainers, you can just pop along to a shoeshop. Easy-peasy. But in the icy Arctic, there aren't many shops around. So the horribly handy Inuit traditionally make all their own clothes. Got a strong stomach? You'll need one for the next bit. You're about to find out how the Inuit make their mukluks (sealskin boots).

Note:
In the past, millions of seals were killed for their fur coats by large-scale seal hunters. But this is now strictly controlled. The Inuit are granted special seal-hunting rights because they need seal meat and fur to survive, and don't simply kill seals for sport or luxury.

1 First the Inuit catch a seal. It's trickier than it looks. Seals spend most of their time in the water, under the ice. Luckily, the Inuit are experts. They know exactly where to find a secretive seal's breathing hole. How? Well, they look for signs of teeth marks in the ice, or they sniff out the seal's strong pong.

2 They wait by the breathing hole, their harpoon ready in their hands. (Today, most Inuit use rifles instead. Unfortunately, they sometimes miss and the loud bang scares the seals away.) They need to be patient. Very patient. It might be hours before the seal comes up for air.

3 Once the seal has been harpooned, it's skinned and the meat is cut into chunks. The Inuit love eating seal, cooked or raw. Dried seal intestines are a particular delicacy. In fact, the only bit of a seal you can't eat is the greasy gall bladder. Any leftovers are deep frozen for winter.

4 The sealskin's stretched out and the blubber's scraped off with a knife. (They don't throw the blubber away – it makes brilliant fuel for lamps and cooking stoves.) Inuit boot-makers take care not to nick the skin, then they soak it in wee, yes, wee, overnight to get it nice and clean. The next step is to rinse it and peg it out to dry.

Please pee on my boots

5 Only now can they start on their boots. They measure their feet and legs with pieces of string. Then they cut out two soles and two uppers from the sealskin. The sealskin's too tough to sew, so they chew it to make it softer. Then they sew the boots together. Traditionally, the Inuit used seal bone needles and seal sinew thread. (Today, people often use dental floss as thread instead!)

CHOMP! CHOMP!

6 They turn the tops over and thread through a drawstring. Now their boots are ready to wear.

Seal souls

One thing the Inuit never forget to do is thank Sedna, the sea goddess, for the seals they catch. They believe that animals have a soul, just like human beings. If you don't show the seal respect, Sedna blows her top. Not a pretty sight. When Sedna's mad, the story goes, her hair gets dirty and matted, and the seals get tangled in it, so there aren't any left to hunt. If this happens, one of the Inuit goes into a deep, deep trance. In his mind's eye, he visits stroppy Sedna's undersea den and combs her hair to set the seals free. Talk about having a bad hair day.

I'M OFF TO SORT OUT SEDNA

Lesson 2: What to eat

OK, so now you've got your polar clothes, what about something to eat? The Arctic's too bloomin' cold to grow fruit and veg, so the Inuit mainly eat fish, fat and meat. And you thought school dinners were boring! Actually, their odd-sounding diet's disgustingly healthy and crammed full of vital vitamins, (unlike your school dinners). After a good day's hunting, the Inuit have a fabulous feast to share out the food they've caught. And guess what? Yep, you're invited.

INUIT FEAST MENU

Starters
• *A selection of delicious dips*
Served with slices of freeze-dried seal or caribou meat.

Dip 1 Tender morsels of lean caribou or seal, mixed with blood and melted fat. Seasoned with ptarmigan (a type of bird) intestine.

Dip 2 Chunks of seal or whale blubber stored in a cool place until it rots and turns into liquid.

Dip 3 The half-digested contents of a caribou's stomach. Pick out any clumps of grass and leaves.

Main course

• Kiviak (kee-vee-yak).

A type of sausage, with a tasty twist. It's a delicacy in Greenland, especially at weddings. Here's the recipe, if you fancy making it at home:

What you need:

• about 300 little auks (tiny seabirds)

• a sealskin, still lined with blubber

What you do:

1 Stuff the sealskin with the little auks, then sew it up.

2 Bury it under a pile of rocks and leave it to rot.

3 Wait for six months, then dig it up again.

4 If it stinks like smelly cheese, it's ready to eat!

Note: *Eat the kiviak with your fingers, taking care to pick out any feathers, bones and beaks that might get stuck in your teeth.*

Optional side dishes

*   *Narwhal (a type of whale) skin strips*
Chewy, with a nice, nutty taste.
*   *Mashed seal brain*
Served warm.
*   *Succulent lichen*
Cut from a caribou's stomach.

Pudding

*   *Caribou surprise*
Forget spotted dick and custard. This pungent pudding is made from blood warmed in a freshly-killed caribou's stomach. Bet that's a surpise to you!

Horrible Health Warning
If you fancy liver and onions, make sure the liver isn't from a polar bear. It contains massive amounts of Vitamin A which can be lethal for human beings.

Lesson 3: Finding shelter

Today, many Inuit live in small, wooden houses in modern towns. Traditionally, they lived in sealskin tents in summer and, in winter, in stone and earth homes built underground. But what if you're out on a hunting trip and a blizzard starts to blow? You need a warm, windproof shelter for a night or two, but there's nothing except snow for miles around. Don't panic, help is at hand. Here's how to build an igloo, or snow house, the most famous type of Inuit shelter of all.

What you need:
*   a knife (made from bone or walrus ivory) or a saw
*   some nice firm snow

What you do:

1 Lie down in the snow and stretch your arms and legs out. Draw a big circle around you by moving your arms and legs up and down (like making a snow "angel").

2 Cut out about 30 blocks of snow, each one about the size of a large suitcase.

3 Lay some of the blocks in a circle, then build up more blocks in a spiral to make a dome shape.

207

4 Fit a final block on top but leave a hole for ventilation.

5 Plug any cracks with snow.

6 Cut an entrance tunnel in one side, below the level of the floor (this stops cold air getting in).

Top tip: Snow's a brilliant material for building with because it traps heat. Inside your igloo, you'll be warm and snug, no matter how perishing cold it is outside. By the way, it takes an expert Inuit builder less than an hour to put up a perfect igloo. How long do you think it would take you?

The Inuit have lived in the Arctic for thousands of years, using their amazing survival skills. But today their lives are changing. Many Inuit have been forced to give up their ancient nomadic lifestyle and move into settlements with mod cons instead. Some of these have made the Inuit's life easier, like supermarkets, rifles and motorized snowmobiles. But some people are worried about their traditional lifestyle dying out. And that would be a terrible tragedy. But it isn't all doom and gloom: some Inuit are fighting back. In 1999, a new territory was created in northern Canada. It's called Nunavut (Noo-na-voot) which means "Our Land" and it's run by and for the Inuit.

South Pole science

Meanwhile, at the South Pole, it's a different story. You see, it's too perishing cold to live there permanently. But you could always spend your hols there (it's costly so you'll need to start saving up, see page 237 for how to get there), or you could work there as a scientist. Amazingly, thousands of long-suffering scientists and support staff work in Antarctica, despite the cold and wind. So why on Earth do they do it? Well, Antarctica's an unbelievably brilliant place for science. For a start, it's the biggest laboratory in the world. And there's nowhere else on the planet like it. But this isn't the sort of science you study at school – you know, the seriously boring sort you can't stay awake in. No, this is science like never before. It's horribly exciting. Forget dull-as-ditchwater experiments and tedious test tubes. This is all about groovy glaciers, deep-frozen fossils, weird wildlife and lots more. Cool, or what?

Could you be a perishing polar scientist?

Do you have what it takes to work at the Poles? Try this quick quiz to see if you're suitable:

1 Are you frightfully fit and healthy? Yes/No
2 Do you like going camping? Yes/No
3 Are you always hungry? Yes/No
4 Do you look good in goggles? Yes/No
5 Are you easy going? Yes/No
6 Are you good at languages? Yes/No
7 Do you hate having a bath? Yes/No

8 Are you neat and tidy? Yes/No
9 Do you have beard?
Yes/No

How did you do?

7–9 yeses: Congratulations! You've really kept your cool. You'll make a brilliant beaker (that's scientists' code for a, er, scientist).

4–6 yeses: Not bad. But perhaps you'd be better off doing something less d–ice–y instead.

3 yeses and below: Oh dear! Polar science is not for you. Try something less adventurous altogether. Something like your geography homework!

OK all you beakers out there, you've done really well and you probably think you're a dead cert for a job. But that was just first base. Check out what you're really letting yourself in for below…

1 Fit and healthy? You'll need to be – there's a lot of hard slog involved in polar science. You'll be given a thorough medical examination before you're allowed to go. Being sporty helps. Rock climbing's especially useful for rescuing people from crevasses (huge cracks in the ice). Mind you don't fall in.

2 Fond of camping? You'd better get used to it. In Antarctica, scientists mostly live on research stations. Some are like small towns with living quarters, science labs, kitchens, hospital, library, gym and their own electricity supply. One station's even got a bowling alley. But scientists also spend months out on freezing field trips where camping's a must. A pyramid tent's best to take because its shape is great in strong winds. But don't forget to mark your camp-site with a flag. Just in case a blizzard blows in and buries it in snow.

3 Always hungry? In Antarctica you burn loads of energy simply keeping warm. Not to mention all the hard work you'll have to do. So you need plenty to eat. In fact, on field trips scientists scoff about 3,500 calories a day – that's twice what you'd normally eat. The food's mostly freeze-dried so it's light and easy to lug about. You simply mix it with water (made from melted ice) and bingo, you've got lunch. Some stations have their own greenhouses so they can grow fresh salad and veg.

4 Look good in goggles? Like it or not, you'll need to wear them to protect your eyes from the sun's glare. It's especially strong in Antarctica because it reflects off the ice and snow. Without goggles or strong sunglasses, you could get snow-blindness and not be able to see for hours, or even days. Nasty. But goggles aren't all you'll need to wear. If you're going to be a serious polar scientist, you'll need serious polar gear. Forget flapping about in a grubby white coat, like your barking mad science teacher – you need to wrap up warm. So what is the serious polar scientist wearing these days? Here's Gloria again with more freezing fashions.

GOGGLES: TO PROTECT YOUR EYES FROM THE SUN'S GLARE AND FROM WIND-BLOWN SNOW

THIN FLEECY TOP: WORN OVER YOUR UNDIES. FLEECE IS A FLUFFY FABRIC MADE OUT OF PLASTIC FIBRES AND IS BRILLIANTLY LIGHT AND WARM

RUCKSACK: FOR CARRYING YOUR SPARE CLOTHES AND FIRST-AID KIT

THERMAL UNDIES: LONG JOHNS AND LONG-SLEEVED VEST WORN NEXT TO YOUR SKIN

FLEECY FACE MASK AND FUR-LINED HOOD: TO STOP YOUR BREATH FREEZING ON YOUR SKIN

SALOPETTES AND JACKET: A TWO-PIECE OUTFIT FILLED WITH DOWN (A BIT LIKE WEARING YOUR DUVET). THEY'RE WINDPROOF, WATERPROOF AND WELL INSULATED, AND WILL KEEP YOU WARM AND SNUG. IT'S ALSO 'BREATHABLE'. THIS MEANS IT LETS SWEAT ESCAPE SO YOUR CLOTHES DON'T GET SODDEN AND FREEZE

GLOVES: YOU'LL NEED TWO PAIRS. WEAR A THIN PAIR OF THERMAL GLOVES UNDERNEATH WITH FLEECE-LINED MITTENS ON TOP

MUKLUKS (BOOTS): MADE FROM RUBBER WITH A CANVAS TOP, WITH THICK, RIDGED RUBBER SOLES SO YOU DON'T SLIP. IT'S BEST TO WEAR THERMAL LINERS INSIDE YOUR BOOTS AND SEVERAL PAIRS OF THICK, THERMAL SOCKS

OR YOU COULD WEAR STURDY CLIMBING BOOTS MADE FROM STRONG, LIGHT PLASTIC. STRAP CRAMPONS (METAL SPIKES) TO THE SOLES TO GET A GRIP ON THE ICE

Note: Like the horribly hardy Inuit, Antarctic scientists wear layers of clothes. These are brilliant at trapping warm air and you can take them off if you get too hot (yes, it can happen). This outfit should keep you warm even if the temperature plummets to a f-f-freezing –40°C.

HORRIBLE HEALTH WARNING

In Antarctica, it's vital to wrap up warm. Otherwise you might end up with fatal frostbite. It attacks your fingers, toes, ears and nose. First they feel prickly, then they go numb. Then they swell up and turn red. And then they go black and drop off. Horrible.

Hypothermia's another horrible hazard. Symptoms include shivering, sluggishness and slurring your words. Eventually, your body temperature drops so much you lose consciousness and can even die.

5 Easy going? You'll need to be. OK, so going to Antarctica's an amazing adventure but it does have its downside. For starters, you'll be stuck on a station for months on end, cut off from the outside world. The dark, the cold and the cramped conditions could easily get on your nerves. Not to mention your fellow suffering scientists.

Trouble is, if things get really bad, you can't just pop outside for a stroll. So you've got to stay chilled. If you get horribly homesick, you can always send an email home.

6 Good at languages? It helps. Science is full of baffling words which can be appallingly long and confusing. To muddle matters even more, polar scientists have their own secret code. I mean, what on Earth are these two talking about?

(Rough translation)
Dingle day – a beautiful day
Jolly – a fun camping trip
Smoko – a tea–break
Bog chisel – a metal stick for checking sea ice
Gash – rubbish

7 Allergic to baths? If baths bring you out in a rash, here's some great news. You can go for days without washing in Antarctica and no one will know you pong. That's because smells are made from tiny particles floating in the moist air. But you can't smell a thing in Antarctica – the air's too

desperately dry. Besides, if you're on a field trip, there aren't going to be any bathrooms. So if you want to go to the toilet, you'll have to dig yourself an, er, ig-loo. It's a big pit in the snow, complete with a loo seat. Don't forget to take everything with you when you leave camp. And that includes any turdicles. Yep, they're like giant icicles but you can guess what they're made from.

8 Neat and tidy? You'll need to be. Everything you need in Antarctica has to be brought by plane or ship. That means food, clothes, building materials, scientific instruments, beds, curtains – you get the picture. And you have to take all your rubbish away with you. Rubbish used to be dumped in the sea or buried under the snow. Today, it's shipped home to be recycled or burned. Otherwise, all this pollution might have a fatal effect on Antarctica's unique landscape and wildlife.

9 Growing a beard? Not essential, but it helps you to look the part. A beard will also keep your face warm, but mind it doesn't freeze. Wear a false beard if you don't have a real one.

Scientists wanted – apply now

Still keen on becoming a polar scientist? Now you've got to decide what sort of scientist you want to be. Take a peek at these pages from the special Antarctic edition of the *Daily Globe* to pick the perfect job for you.

Daily Globe — JOB HUNT

GLORIOUS OPPORTUNITIES FOR GLACIOLOGISTS!

JOB DESCRIPTION:
If you like ice, this is the job for you. You'll spend most of your time knee deep in the stuff.

SKILLS REQUIRED:
You'll need to be able to tell how old ice is by drilling out ice cores and studying them (see pages 171–172), using high-tech equipment.

WE'LL PROVIDE:
radars and satellites to help you work out how much ice there is, and how fast it's melting.

BRILLIANT BASE FOR BIOLOGISTS!

JOB DESCRIPTION:
You'll enjoy studying how living things survive at the Poles, without freezing to death.

SKILLS REQUIRED:
Must be prepared to tackle everything from tracking albatrosses by satellite to scuba diving under the frozen sea to follow fish and seals.

WE'LL PROVIDE:
equipment for drilling miles and miles down through the ice to study bacteria recently discovered in ancient lakes. We need someone to work out how they got there…

MUST HAVE – METEOROLOGISTS!

JOB DESCRIPTION: You'll love braving the bone-chilling cold to find out all about the polar weather, and forecast the weather around the world.

SKILLS REQUIRED:
You'll need to be a whizz at maths. There's lots of checking equipment and long sums involved.

WE'LL PROVIDE:
satellite equipment, so you can monitor the size of the hole in the ozone layer, recently discovered by polar scientists. (See Poles in Peril for the hole, sorry whole story.) We'll also provide automatic weather stations.

Great jobs for go-ahead-GEOLOGISTS!

JOB DESCRIPTION:
You'll be able to find out about the Earth by looking at rotten rocks. After tracking the rocks down, that is. You'll also study how glaciers grind rocks down.
SKILLS REQUIRED:
As you know, most of the land in Antarctica's buried under ice. You'll also need an eye for precious metals – there are small amounts of gold, silver and other metals hidden in some of the rocks. You'll also study volcanoes – hope you're feeling brave. In 1969, a volcano on Deception Island blew its top, destroying two nearby scientific stations.
WE'LL PROVIDE:
radar and satellites for you to peek at the peaks underneath.

PERFECT POSITIONS FOR PALAEONTOLOGISTS!

JOB DESCRIPTION:

You'll love studying fossils in the rocks to find out what life was like long ago. You might find fossils of plants, reptiles and even long-dead dinosaurs.

SKILLS REQUIRED:

You'll be able to compare crucial fossil clues with similar fossils found in other parts of the world, to unearth the history of the polar regions. Worth knowing that scientists have already worked out that Antarctica was once toasty and warm, and part of a massive supercontinent. (See page 157 for the heart-warming details.)

WE'LL PROVIDE:

tools for getting the fossils and transport for lugging them home (so you won't have to drag a sledge full of rocks like Captain Scott and his men).

ASTOUNDING ADVENTURES FOR ASTRONOMERS!

JOB DESCRIPTION:

You'll be tracking the sun with telescopes, along with other stars and planets. You'll also be on the lookout for masses of meteorites (lumps of space rock), lying around on the ice.

SKILLS REQUIRED:

Must be able to handle other excited astronomers who've recently found loads of meteorites. They believe that the rocks are millions of years old and come from the moon and from Mars. Astronomers also study the aurorae (see page 158) and space weather (rays from outer space which reach the Earth). Space storms can knock out satellites, cause power black-outs and be desperately dangerous for astronauts on space walks from the space shuttle.

WE'LL PROVIDE:

incredibly clear air to make your job as easy as pie and, in summer, all-day sunshine. So keeping track of the sun will be a breeze.

So, you're armed with your new-found knowledge of the perishing Poles. You think you've found your ideal job and you've packed your false beard. But, hang on a minute, before you get too big for your sealskin boots, spare a thought for those plucky polar pioneers who didn't make the grade. For years, intrepid explorers have set off to find out what the fuss was all about. Only some of them lived to tell the teeth-chattering tale...

Some people like skating on very thin ice. Or sailing close to the wind. A nice, quiet life in front of the telly would bore them to tears. Nope, they want excitement and adventure. And they'll go to the ends of the Earth for it. Despite the dreadful dangers, people have been exploring the perishing Poles for years. They've braved icebergs, blizzards and polar bears. But what on Earth did they do it for? Some of them were in it for money. They wanted to open the Poles up for trade. Others simply wanted to see bits of the world no one had ever seen before. Besides, being a polar explorer was seen as a dead glamorous job. Fame and fortune were guaranteed. If you made it back alive, that is.

Early explorers
First reports from the far north
In about 325 BC, a globe-trotting Greek, Pytheas, set sail on an astonishing voyage. He spent years sailing across the North Atlantic and exploring the frozen north. He even got as far as Iceland, or so he said. Sadly, when he finally got back home again, nobody believed him. You could say they gave poor Pytheas the cold shoulder. People laughed when he said

he'd seen seas covered in ice that shook like wobbly jelly. A likely tale, they said. (In fact, geographers now know this was pancake ice.)

WAS THERE CUSTARD AS WELL?

And they sniggered at his description of a place where the sun shone all night in summer but didn't rise in winter. (They'd never heard of the midnight sun, you see.) Pytheas spent the rest of his life trying to convince people he wasn't fibbing.

Adventurous Vikings

But it was really the adventurous Vikings who put the Arctic on the map. In about AD 982, a vicious Viking called Erik the Red went to live in Greenland. (He had to flee from Iceland where he was wanted for a bloody murder.) Of course, it wasn't called Greenland then. Enterprising Erik made up the name to trick other Vikings into going with him. And guess what? It worked a treat. Greenland sounded so, well, er, green, that people happily packed up and went. Goodness knows what they thought when they got there, faced with freezing cold weather and awesome icebergs.

GREENLAND

IF IT'S NOT GREEN, IT'S NOT HERE!

SCANDINAVIAN TOURIST BOARD AD 982

Despite the hostile conditions, the hardy Vikings flourished for almost 500 years. They farmed the land and kept sheep, goats and cattle. Gradually, they disappeared – no one knows why. Some people think they were kidnapped by pirates or died from the plague. But experts reckon there was a sudden cold snap and the Vikings froze to death. Trouble is, their clothes weren't warm enough and they didn't know how to hunt for food. So when the cold weather killed their crops, the unlucky Vikings starved. If only they'd asked the local people for some life-saving survival tips.

Into the unknown

Meanwhile, at the other end of the Earth, Antarctica was still a mystery, even though the ancient Greeks guessed it was there. On early maps, it was labelled *Terra Australis Incognita*, which means "unknown southern land". But no one had ever been there.

Then, in 1772, go-getting English explorer, Captain James Cook (1728–1779), sailed off in search of the fabled continent. James didn't actually see it but he crossed the

Antarctic Circle for the first time and sailed right round Antarctica before pack ice forced him back. Bitterly disappointed, Cook wrote glumly in his diary:

The greater part of such a continent must lie within the Polar Circle, where the sea is so pestered with ice that the land is inaccessible. Thick fogs, snow storms, intense cold ... are heightened by the inexpressibly horrid aspect of the country, doomed by nature to lie buried under everlasting ice and snow.

As far as he was concerned, he added gloomily, Antarctica was of no use to anyone.

In fact, the first person to set foot on Antarctica was probably an American, John Davis. He landed in February 1821 to hunt for seals. And that sealed his fate, you could say.

Earth-shattering fact

When Captain Cook died, his friends put on a pantomime in London to celebrate his globe-trotting life. But forget boring pantomime horses. In honour of Cook's Antarctic adventures, a specially made mini iceberg stole the show.

AND NOW FOR MY FIRST TRICK

Teacher teaser

Everyone knows that Amundsen reached the South Pole first but what about the nippy North Pole? Test your teacher's polar know-how with this harmless-sounding question. Stick up your hand and say:

PLEASE, MISS, WHO REACHED THE NORTH POLE FIRST?

ER...ER...

Answer: Sorry, this is a trick question. You see, the answer depends on whose story you believe. While your teacher's making her mind up, we've dug out an old copy of the *Daily Globe* to fill you in on the real-life details...

The Daily Globe
NEW YORK, USA
TOP EXPLORERS IN POLAR PUNCH-UP

Bitter controversy raged today as not one but two of our best-known explorers claimed the honour of being the first person at the North Pole. Yesterday, we received the sensational news that Commander Robert Peary of the US Navy had braved frostbite and biting blizzards to conquer the North Pole. He reached the Pole on 6 April. For Peary, 53, it was a dream come true and this doughty polar veteran was understandably thrilled.

"My life's work is accomplished," he told our reporter. "I have got the North Pole out of my system after 23 years of effort, hard work, disappointments, hardships, privations, more or less suffering, and some risks. I have won the last great geographical prize, the North Pole, for the credit of the United States… I am content."

With two failed attempts behind him, it was third time lucky for plucky Peary. He put his success down to months spent learning essential Inuit survival skills. At the Pole, Peary and his companions hoisted an American flag and posed for a photo.

PEARY'S POLE

The flag was made by Peary's wife, Josephine.

PROUD MOMENT

"The bitter wind burned our faces so that they cracked," Commander Peary told us. "The air was keen and bitter as frozen steel."

A heroic feat indeed.

Or was it? No sooner had the news broken than the story took an extraordinary turn. As Peary's news reached home, his bitter rival, Dr Frederick Cook was celebrating his discovery of the North Pole at a banquet in Copenhagen. A one-time travelling companion of Peary, Dr Cook has just returned from a two-year expedition to the Arctic. Incredibly, he claims to have reached the Pole on 21 April 1908, a whole year before Peary.

JUST WHAT THE DOCTOR ORDERED

When Cook was told of Peary's achievement, he replied graciously. "If he has announced he has reached the farthest North, he has," Cook said. "There is honour enough on it for both of us."

The question is: which of these two intrepid explorers is telling the truth. Who should we believe? Will it be proud Peary or courageous Cook who claims his place in history? The story looks set to run and run. *The Daily Globe* will keep you up-to-date with all the latest developments.

In pole position

When Peary heard Cook's claim, he was furious. You can understand why. He called Cook a liar and vowed to find out the truth. Unluckily for Peary, the public were on Cook's side. Cheering crowds welcomed him home with "WE BELIEVE YOU!" banners.

Both men had their diaries and notebooks examined by learned geographical societies who eventually ruled in Peary's favour, even though there wasn't any real proof. Trouble is, Cook's dates didn't add up, they said. And the piece of land he claimed to have seen didn't actually exist. Worse still, crafty Cook has already been proved a fibber. A few years before, he claimed to have climbed Mount McKinley in Alaska (the highest peak in North America) for the first time. In fact, his photos later turned out to be fakes. Cook was expelled from the Explorers' Club of New York and spent the rest of his life in disgrace.

So was Peary telling the truth? It was difficult to tell. Some people reckoned he'd made it all up. After all, they said, there was no way he could have got to the Pole and back as quickly as he claimed.

Who do you believe?

P-p-p-pick your own polar explorer

Picture the scene. You're stranded at the perishing Poles and you're allowed one person to keep you company. But who should you choose? They'll need to be brave, tough and determined, and ice-cool in an emergency. Each of the polar pioneers below have proved they're intrepid explorers. All you have to do is pick the one you think's the pluckiest. Here's Gloria to introduce our five daring contestants...

Each of our contestants has already pitted their survival skills against the perishing Poles. But now it's your turn to choose one of them to be your travelling companion.

Make sure you're equipped for the trip of a lifetime by listening carefully to their case histories before you choose...

Contestant no. 1
NAME: Willem Barents (1550?–1597)
NATIONALITY: Dutch
CLAIM TO FAME: Brave Barents made three daring voyages in search of a new sea route to Asia across the north of Siberia. When his ship got stuck in the ice, he became the first European to spend winter in the freezing Arctic. Brrrr!
SPECIAL SKILLS: Building a house out of a shipwreck. To pick weather-beaten Willem, vote for contestant number 1.

Contestant no. 2
NAME: Sir John Franklin (1786–1847)
NATIONALITY: British
CLAIM TO FAME: Salty old sea dog, Sir John had travelled the world. He spent years sailing in the Arctic in search of a new sea route to Asia across the north of Canada. OK, so he didn't find it but he got his own statue in Westminster Abbey in London. So there.
SPECIAL SKILLS: A brilliant navigator and sailor.
To pick seaworthy Sir John, vote for contestant number 2.

Contestant no. 3
NAME: Salomon Andrée (1854–1897)
NATIONALITY: Swedish
CLAIM TO FAME: Attempted to become the first person to fly to the North Pole in a hot-air balloon. The balloon was called the Eagle. Salomon was so famous he had his waxwork displayed at Madame Tussaud's in London. Now that's cool!
SPECIAL SKILLS: Mad about flying.
To pick high-flying Salomon, vote for contestant number 3.

230

Contestant no. 4
NAME: Knud Rasmussen (1879–1933)
NATIONALITY: Danish/Inuit
CLAIM TO FAME: Clever Knud was the first person to study how the Inuit people lived and survived in the icy Arctic. They taught Knud everything he knew and he became a top polar expert.
SPECIAL SKILLS: Hunting, fishing, driving dog sledges.
To pick knowledgeable Knud, vote for contestant number 4.

Contestant no. 5
NAME: Sir Douglas Mawson (1882–1958)
NATIONALITY: Australian
CLAIM TO FAME: Brilliant scientist Sir Douglas led the Australasian Antarctic Expedition in 1911. He explored an unknown stretch of coast and found the first Antarctic meteorite.
SPECIAL SKILLS: Toughness and determination.
To pick daring Sir Douglas, vote for contestant number 5.

So which of these cool customers did you choose? You're about to find out if you'll survive the journey. Here are the results in reverse order...

5 If you chose contestant number 2, you're lost. Hopelessly lost. Sir John might have been brilliant at navigating at sea but on land it was another story. In 1845, Sir John set sail for the Arctic with 128 men. And was never heard from again. His worried wife offered a £20,000 reward (a fortune in those days) and sent out several search parties. Her husband was nowhere to be found. Finally, in 1859, the searchers found a note hidden under a pile of stones. It said daring Sir John had died in 1847, trying to fetch help.

4 If you chose contestant number 3, you'll survive but only for three months. In 1897, Salomon and two companions took off from Spitsbergen in Norway to fly to the North Pole. But just three days after take-off, the balloon got weighed down with ice and was forced to crash-land. The three men survived for three months on a diet of polar bear meat. But, sadly, all three perished. It was only in 1930 that their bodies were finally found and their tragic story pieced together from their diaries and photos. (To make matters worse, Salomon's waxwork was eaten by mice.)

3 If you chose contestant number 1, you'll be OK, but you might have trouble getting back. Worthy Willem was cool as a cucumber in a crisis, and horribly practical, too. When his ship got stuck, did he panic? Did he, heck! He coolly built a cosy hut on the ice, out of the ship's timbers. It even had a bath tub, made out of an old wine cask. And instead of hot-water bottles, the men took hot stones to bed instead. Unfortunately, Willem didn't make it back. In summer, he tried to sail for home but died from scurvy. (Though most of his men survived.)

2 If you chose contestant number 4, you'll be in safe hands, though you might die from food poisoning. Cool Knud grew up in Greenland. As a kid, he learned how to hunt, fish and drive a dog sledge like an Inuit. He could also speak several Inuit languages. What a swot! Knud later went to Denmark to train as an opera singer. But he was soon back in Greenland where he set up a bank instead. He used the money he made from banking to fund more expeditions. (Knud eventually died from food poisoning caused by eating a bad pickled auk.)

I But the winner is ... Contestant number 5. You'll definitely survive with fearless Douglas. In fact, he'll probably outlast you. Gutsy Sir Douglas Mawson showed just how to survive against all the odds. While out on a sledging trip, one of his companions suddenly disappeared down a crevasse, taking his sledge, dogs, tent and all their food down with him. Then his other companion died from food poisoning (by this time, they'd been forced to eat the rest of the dogs). Half-dead himself, Sir Douglas struggled on alone. Somehow he made it back to camp ... just in time to see his ship sailing away! He was forced to spend another winter in Antarctica. Congratulations, Sir Douglas! Talk about keeping your cool.

HI MUM!

So congratulations to those of you who picked our worthy winner. Your special prize is a thrilling dog sledge ride to the North Pole. Yes, you'll soon be hurtling across the ice at full speed ... pulled by a pack of pooches! Don't panic. They're brilliant at spotting crevasses (usually). Just one thing before you set off. We've left it to you to set the sledge up.

Drive a dog sledge

What you need:

- a wooden sledge
- about five to ten huskies

What you do:

1 Round up your huskies. Huskies are horribly hardy dogs, perfectly suited to polar travel. (They also make brilliant pets – if you can get them off your sofa.) They've got thick, woolly coats to keep them warm, and they're super–strong (a team of ten huskies can pull you and a fully loaded sledge 50 kilometres a day).

SORE THROAT? | NO, I'M JUST A LITTLE HUSKY

And you can feed huskies on seal blubber if you've forgotten to bring the tin opener. (By the way, they go to sleep curled up in the snow, so there's no need for a dog kennel.)

2 Hitch your huskies to your sledge, in a fan formation. Each dog has a specially padded harness which goes round its chest (not round its neck like an ordinary dog collar). Fix them to the sledge by nylon ropes called traces. Let the strongest, most intelligent dog take the lead. The traces spread out in a fan shape. So if the lead dog falls into a crevasse, the others won't follow (you hope).

3 Stand on the back of the sledge. Call "*Hike! Hike!*" – that's the command to get the dogs moving. (Other useful commands include: *Gee* – turn right; *Haw* – turn left; *Straight on* – go straight; *Easy* – slow down; *Whoa* – stop; and *On-by* – put that rabbit down.)

Now you're really mushing (that's the technical term for driving a dog sledge).

(Important note: to brake, stand on the metal bar between the sledge runners and push it down into the snow.)

4 If your dogs get tired (should that be dog tired?), you'll need to pedal the sledge yourself. That means pushing the sledge forward with one foot, as if you're riding a scooter. Don't worry if you keep falling off – mushing takes years of practice. But once you get the hang of it, it's a horribly thrilling ride. *Hike! Hike!*

Note: You can't go mushing in Antarctica. Since 1994, dogs have been banned. Scientists thought they had distemper (a deadly disease) and might spread it to the seals.

Modern-day exploration

If all this talk of adventure has given you itchy feet, why not explore the perishing poles yourself? Each year, hundreds of people set off for the poles. But if mushing isn't your cup of tea, there are lots of other exciting ways of getting about. You could hitch a lift on an aeroplane (many polar planes have skis instead of wheels so they can land safely on the ice) or take a cruise in an icebreaker (a specially strengthened steel ship for smashing through the ice). You could even go by submarine. In 1958, an American sub, *Nautilus*, reached the North Pole by travelling all the way under the ice.

Unlike explorers of the past, modern explorers have lots of mod cons to help them. They use radios and email to keep in touch and satellites to help them navigate. Even then, exploring the perishing Poles is a horribly risky thing to do. With day-long darkness and white-outs, it's easy to get hoplessly lost. Dead lost. After a while, one ice floe looks much the same as another and there aren't any handy road signs around. If this happens, you might like to take a leaf out of the local Inuits' book. They use the sun or the pattern made by the wind in the snow to help them find their way. Whatever you do, never fix your route from an iceberg. It'll keep drifting off to sea...

POLES IN PERIL

But apart from exploring, what on Earth can you use a perishing Pole for? I mean, the Poles are just piles of useless old ice stuck miles away from anywhere, aren't they? Wrong. Hidden under the ice and the frozen seas are some really useful polar riches. Trouble is, horrible humans are so busy trying to get them out that they're putting the fragile Poles at risk. So why are the Poles in peril? Here are five precious polar prizes and how horrible humans might be spoiling them.

Polar prize 1: Fabulous fur seals

What we're doing: In the 18th and 19th centuries in Antarctica, millions of seals were killed for their fur. It was used to make fancy fur hats, coats, slippers and felt cloth for fashionable ladies in Europe, America and China.

Elephant seals were also clobbered to death for their blubber (which was boiled down to make high-quality oil) and walruses were killed for their ivory.

What's wrong with that? So many seals were slaughtered that some species were almost wiped out. Pretty grim, eh? The good news is, large-scale hunting of some seals is now completely banned, though local people can still catch a few for food. Since the hunting stopped, seal stocks have quickly recovered and the seals are now protected.

Polar prize 2: Whopping whales

What we're doing: And it wasn't just the seals the hunters were after. Millions of whales were killed for their meat, blubber and whalebone. It was used for making combs, fishing rods, umbrellas and posh ladies' corsets. Even 100 years ago a whalebone from a large-ish whale could fetch a whopping £2,500. Whale hunting was big business.

What's wrong with that? At one time, whales were hunted almost to extinction. And they're still pretty rare. Today, though, there are strict rules to protect the whales from harm. A few hundred whales can be killed each year for food or scientific research. But commercial hunting is banned. In 1994, Antarctica and the Southern Ocean were officially declared a Whale Sanctuary. And whopping whales are making a come-back.

Polar prize 3: Deep-freeze fish

What we're doing: Fishing fleets catch million of tonnes of fish, krill and squid each year from polar seas. Modern trawlers are horribly high-tech. They use computers, radar and satellites to track the seafood down, and enormous nets to catch it. Some are like floating fish factories. They can clean, freeze and can fish on board. Handy, eh?

What's wrong with that? Some fishermen are breaking the rules about how many fish they can catch. That's bad luck for Patagonian toothfish. Their tasty meat makes them a very valuable catch. Trouble is, it takes a toothfish about 30 years to reach adult size (about 2 metres). And so many fish are being caught (illegally), they don't have time to catch up. To make matters worse, thousands of seabirds, like albatrosses, get tangled up in the fishing lines.

HAVE YOU BEEN NEAR THAT FISHING BOAT AGAIN?

WHO? ME?

Polar prize 4: Oodles of oil

What we're doing: There's oodles of precious oil under the Arctic ice and tundra. And horrible humans are digging deep to get it out. Serious supplies of oil have already been found in icy Siberia and Alaska. It's pumped out of the ground and piped thousands of miles to an oil refinery.

So what's wrong with that? Well, the roads and pipes lines used to transport the oil are spoiling the fragile polar habitat. Take the plight of the Arctic National Wildlife Refuge in Alaska. It's the largest national park in the USA but it may soon be history. That's if the US government goes ahead with its plans to drill for oil. Then there's the risk of oil spills. In 1989, the oil tanker, *Exxon Valdez*, ran aground off the coast of Alaska, spilling 50 million litres of oil into the sea. That's enough to fill 13 Olympic-sized swimming pools.

And that's an awful lot of oil. A huge stretch of coast was soaked in oil, and thousands of fish, birds and sea mammals were killed. There may be loads of oil off the Antarctic coast, too, but it's horribly hard to find. Besides, commercial mining of any sort is banned in Antarctica until at least the year 2041.

Polar prize 5: Horrible holidays
What we're doing: Every year, thousands of tourists head for the perishing Poles. Believe it or not. Fancy a horrible holiday?

Horrible Holidays

are proud to present their

PERISHING POLAR ☆ CRUISE ☆

FED UP WITH LOUNGING ABOUT ON THE BEACH?

TIRED OF BORING DAYS OUT AT THE ZOO?

FANCY A HOLIDAY ON ICE?

BOOK NOW **PLACES LIMITED**

FOR THE COOLEST HOLIDAY AROUND, TREAT YOURSELF TO OUR PERISHING POLAR CRUISE. THE TOUR THAT TAKES YOU TO THE ENDS OF THE EARTH. PRICE INCLUDES TRANSPORT BY ICE BREAKER AND INFLATABLE BOAT, AND THE SERVICES OF A TOP POLAR GUIDE. IT'S THE HOLIDAY THAT REALLY TAKES YOU AWAY FROM IT ALL.

SMALL PRINT.

DON'T FORGET TO BRING A GOOD BOOK. IF THE WEATHER'S BAD YOU MIGHT BE STUCK ON BOARD FOR DAYS ON END. AND THERE'S ONLY SO MANY SHOTS OF ICEBERGS YOU CAN SNAP AND TAKE HOME TO BORE YOUR FRIENDS WITH.

What's wrong with that? Some people think tourists might be doing more harm than good. Especially if they disturb the local wildlife and leave loads of litter behind. On the other hand, if they go home and tell other people how amazingly cool the perishing Poles can be, it might help to save them.

If you're heading for Antarctica on holiday, here are some simple dos and don'ts for keeping the Poles in peak condition.

DO...
• Keep your distance from the birds and seals. Especially when you're taking their piccy. If they notice you, you're too close. Never feed or touch them.
• Take all your litter home with you. Don't chuck anything overboard from your cruise ship.
• Check with any research station before you pay them a visit. You might get in the scientists' way.

DON'T...
• Walk on any lichens, mosses or flowers. They're horribly delicate and will take years to grow back again.
• Collect any rocks, fossils or bones as souvenirs.
• Wander off on your own – Antarctica's a perilous place. Stick with your group and keep to set tracks and trails and listen to instructions from your polar guide.
• Walk on glacier or snow fields. You might not spot a lethal crevasse until it's too late.
• Shout! You'll frighten the animals – they're used to peace and quiet.

245

HORRIBLE HEALTH WARNING

In the early 1980s, scientists discovered a huge hole in the ozone layer above the South Pole. Ozone's a horribly useful gas that blocks out the sun's burning ultraviolet rays. Too much of these and you'd be burned to a crisp. Very nasty. And the hole's growing every year. In fact, it's now about twice the size of the hole, sorry, whole, of Europe.

Guess who was to blame? Yep, horrible humans, of course. For years, we'd been dumping tonnes of ghastly gases called CFCs (chlorofluorocarbons) into the atmosphere. They were used in fridges, foam and aerosol sprays (like spray-on deodorants). Luckily, we're cleaning up our act and CFCs have been banned. (By the way, this doesn't mean you have to pong. These days most deodorants are CFC-free.) But CFCs take a long time to disappear from the atmosphere. It will take at least 50 years for the ozone hole to mend.

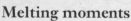

Melting moments

But if you really fancy a holiday on ice, you'd better get your skates on. What's the rush? Well, horrible geographers are worried that the perishing Poles are melting because the Earth's getting warmer. Already, huge chunks of ice are breaking off Antarctica, and the Arctic sea ice is shrinking. The question is: are humans to blame this time or is it down to nasty nature? Time to call the experts in. The only problem is finding two horrible geographers that agree – about anything!

It's people who are to blame, I'm afraid. We're pumping too many ghastly greenhouse gases* into the atmosphere. And they're making the world warm up at an alarming rate.

* They're gases like carbon dioxide and methane that keep the Earth snug and warm. They work a bit like the glass in your grandad's greenhouse — they let the sun's rays in but stop heat from the Earth escaping. These gases come from exhaust fumes from cars and lorries, pollution from factories and power stations, and from burning too many rainforest trees.

Stuff and nonsense. It's nature to blame. The Earth's climate changes naturally. It never stays the same for long. After all, we've been having cold snaps and warm spells for millions of years.

Even so, most scientists now reckon that horrible humans are to blame for our warming world. They predict that the Earth will heat up by about 2°C by the year 2100. Which might not sound much to you but just a teeny rise in temperature could melt the ice sheets and glaciers at the Poles. If this happened, an awesome amount of water would pour into the sea, raising sea level by 50 metres or more, and drowning many low-lying islands and cities. Watch out if you live in London or Venice – it's going to get horribly soggy.

A PERISHING FUTURE?

So what does the future hold for the perishing Poles? Is it all gloom and doom? The good news is that people are working hard to keep the Poles pristine.

A tricky treaty

At the North Pole, the land is owned by the various Arctic nations. But who owns the South Pole? The answer is: nobody. In 1959, 12 countries signed a historic document called the Antarctic Treaty. It sets out how Antarctica is governed. These countries promised to make sure Antarctica is protected and is used for peaceful purposes only. And the good news is, so far the Treaty seems to be working. Today, 44 countries have signed up. Here's what they've agreed to do:

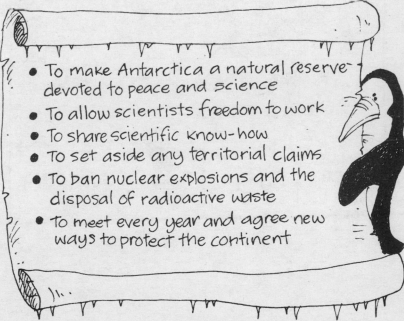

- To make Antarctica a natural reserve devoted to peace and science
- To allow scientists freedom to work
- To share scientific know-how
- To set aside any territorial claims
- To ban nuclear explosions and the disposal of radioactive waste
- To meet every year and agree new ways to protect the continent

In 1998, another bit was added to the Antarctic Treaty. It bans any mining or drilling for oil in Antarctica, and protects Antarctica's unique wildlife. It also says that scientists and tourists must take all their waste away with them, in case it harms the fragile environment. Will this be enough to protect the Pole? We'll just have to wait and see. Some people say that the only way to save the Pole for good is to turn Antarctica into a giant World Park. But they're still arguing about who'd be the park keeper. In the meantime, one thing's for certain. The perishing Poles are amazing wildernesses, with people and animals found nowhere else on Earth. It would be a terrible tragedy if they disappeared. Besides, they're the coolest places on the planet to be. And that's the teeth-chattering truth.

Websites

If you're still interested in finding out more, here are some polar websites you can check out:

www.antarctica.ac.uk
The British Antarctic Survey's website, with up-to-date info and diaries of scientists based in Antarctica.

www.spri.cam.ac.uk
The Scott Polar Research Institute. Info about Arctic people, explorers, landscape and wildlife.

www.south-pole.com
Masses of info about Antarctic explorers, and facts and figures about polar weather.

www.heritage-antarctica.org
The website of the Antarctic Heritage Trust. Join the trust and help save Scott and Shackleton's old expedition huts (you'll also get a copy of its newsletter, *Bergy Bits*).

www.iaato.org
The website of the International Association of Antarctica Tour Operators has information about Antarctic tourism.

www.survival-international.org
Survival International's website. Survival is a worldwide organization helping local people protect their homes and land.

Horrible Geography

Geography with the gritty bits left in!

Also available:

Violent Volcanoes

Odious Oceans

Stormy Weather

Raging Rivers

Desperate Deserts

Earth-shattering Earthquakes

Freaky Peaks

Bloomin' Rainforests

Perishing Poles

Intrepid Explorers

Wild Islands

Monster Lakes

Cracking Coasts